IN THE TRENCHES AT FRONT SIGHT

Brad Ackman

IN THE TRENCHES AT FRONT SIGHT

25 YEARS IN THE FIREARMS TRAINING INDUSTRY WITH BRAD ACKMAN

BRAD ACKMAN

REAL DEAL PUBLICATIONS, LLC

First Edition Published 2012
Second Edition and Second Printing 2013
Third Edition and Third Printing 2014
Fourth Edition and Fourth Printing 2016 by
Real Deal Publications, LLC
150 South Highway 160, Suite #8
PMB #402
Pahrump, NV 89048
www.RealDealPublications.com

ISBN: 978-0-9856825-0-7

Library of Congress Control Number: 2012917430

Photographs and illustrations by Brad Ackman
Cover design by Jim Westbrook

Printed in the U.S.A.

CONTENTS

INTRODUCTION

Y OU will enjoy this book. Unfortunately, in the end, you won't be a better shooter, or a better tactician, and certainly not a better person! There are no training tips and precious few pearls of wisdom. I wrote this book for entertainment value, pure and simple. Some of my experiences in the firearms training world over the last 25 years still make me smile, and are too good to keep to myself. I hope they make you smile, too.

After the first couple of introductory chapters, this book is not divided into categories nor does it follow any particular chronology. Instead, it flows much like a good conversation, meandering from one idea to the next. The individual chapters are concise. We have all slogged through literary works where the author uses 500 words just to tell us "the sun was rising" or "the dog was barking." You won't suffer that same fate here.

There is a very modest amount of swearing in some chapters; sorry about that. I toned it down a lot compared to the original occurrence, but I left in a little bit because that's reality. A friend of mine always held that "Vulgarity is the sign of an inadequate vocabulary." By that standard, I guess my vocabulary failed me a few times while writing the following pages.

On occasion, I took just a touch of artistic license. If you read a passage and say "Hey, he's talking about me," you are probably right. But notice I changed your name to protect your honor!

And what about a Dedication? It seems that every book ever written has one of those. The "Thank You's" generally go out to the wife, the mentor, or God himself. Nothing so lofty here. However, I would like to acknowledge the working stiffs at Front Sight; not only the ones wearing black and gray uniforms, but also the ones wearing leather gloves, steel-toed boots, sweat, and Band Aids.

Enjoy!

Brad Ackman at Front Sight in March 2012.

FROM WHENCE I CAME

To give you as sense of who I am and how my firearms career evolved, I offer you the following timeline.

As a kid growing up in Colorado, I was frequently around guns, thanks to my father's interest in bird hunting. I received no formal training, but really, how hard could it be; point the damn thing and pull the trigger! In April of 1982, I had my big realization; there is actually more to the proper use of guns than simply "point and pull the trigger." I needed proper firearms training. A couple of months later, at age 18 and freshly out of high school, I attended my first defensive handgun course under Jeff Cooper. Jeff was the founder of Gunsite, a firearms training facility in Arizona. Jeff Cooper and Gunsite were the uncontested champions of private firearms training from the late-1970's through the mid-1990's.

In the fall of 1982, I headed off to college at Southern Methodist University. During my stint in Dallas, I became a fairly serious handgun competitor and I continued my training under Jeff Cooper. In June of 1985, I became an Instructor for Jeff Cooper at Gunsite, much to my surprise and delight. This was a part-time deal for me as I was still in college. A Bachelor's degree in May of 1986 proved to my dad that the last four years really had been worth it!

I kind of liked the whole college thing and "employment" seemed so serious and formal. Thus, I enrolled at the University of Montana in Missoula to pursue my Master's degree. During every conceivable break, I was at Gunsite teaching folks the proper use of handguns and shotguns. Ignatius Piazza took his first course under Jeff Cooper in the summer of 1988, which is how I met him.

After securing my Master's degree, I continued north to Alaska. I worked for an environmental engineering firm which amounted to lots of time in remote Alaska, much of it with a flyrod or rifle in hand.

In 1994, Ignatius started this little enterprise known as "Front Sight" and he asked me to serve as the Operations Manager. My formal commitment to Front Sight meant the end of my professional association with Gunsite in Arizona. Front Sight opened its doors in April of 1996 and offered courses at a leased facility in Bakersfield, California. I made the significant commute from Anchorage to Bakersfield twice each month.

To kick-off 1999 in grand style, Front Sight graduated from the temporary, leased facilities in California to our current, permanent location outside of Las Vegas. Our student numbers were really taking off, so I too relocated from Alaska to Nevada to concentrate full-time on Front Sight.

In the summer of 2003, Ignatius announced in a staff meeting that he wanted to open a second location where we could train during the hot summer months. I knew the answer to this one…Alaska! I headed to Alaska in search of land suitable to build a small, seasonal facility. I found the right spot just north of Kenai and we spent that winter building. We opened Front Sight Alaska in the summer of 2004 and I have spent summers there ever since. You will notice a good number of the following stories emanate from Alaska.

I still serve as Front Sight's Operations Manager, helping train untold thousands of good folks every year, and racking-up more humorous stories along the way.

THAT GOT ME THINKING

My big realization came on a cold, snowy day in Littleton, Colorado in late-April of 1982. April was supposed to be warm, but apparently the whole Global Warming thing had not caught on yet. I was just finishing my senior year in high school and I was pretty excited about heading off to college in the fall. I had grown up around guns, as my dad was an enthusiastic duck and goose hunter. However, the closest I had come to formal training was hollering "Pull!" on the trap and skeet range and having people tell me "You're doing it all wrong."

When I walked into the house after school that April day, the phone was already ringing. I answered with the mandated "Ackman residence" because heaven-forbid someone simply say "Hello." My long-time friend Jon was on the other end breathing a little too hard. "What is it?" I asked. "Dan just shot Cameron Garza," he said.

Dan was a family friend who was maybe 10 years older than I was. He graduated from college as a pharmacist and subsequently opened a business just down the street from my house. His business was the ultimate stop-and-rob. It was a combination drug store, convenience store, liquor store, and shipping/mailing store. Something for everyone…pills, booze, cash. Dan was a smart guy and knew the perils of running that sort of business. He kept a Colt Commander in the drawer behind the pharmacy counter, just in case. Dan was a gun enthusiast, but not a gunfighter.

On the other side of this equation was Cameron, a high-school hoodlum. We were seniors together at Littleton High, but Cameron was a few years older than most seniors because he had to revisit a couple of grades along the way. He stemmed from a tough home where he got lots of practice using his fists. Instead of nurturing his athletic talents to best play the hand he was dealt, he preferred the lazy approach of being a scumbag.

Apparently Cameron was having a day worse than others. He had hit rock bottom and decided to take an early exit off the planet. He found his dad's stolen snub-nose .38 and strolled over to the drug store. Cameron walked back to the pharmacy counter where Dan was working. "I want 500 Valium," Cameron said in a determined voice. Dan replied with "If you have a prescription, I'll certainly fill it." "I've got your prescription right here," Cameron said as he dug the .38 out of the pocket of his sweatshirt. Dan quickly found himself looking down the wrong end of Cameron's gun. Dan obliged by scooping a few big handfuls of Valium into the white paper bag. At the same time, he casually slid open the drawer which held the 1911. Cameron snatched the bag out of Dan's hand and turned for the door. He went about seven or eight paces, almost to the front door, and then abruptly spun around and pointed the gun back at Dan. There was no doubt in Dan's mind that now was the time, so he grabbed the 1911 and fired a single shot. Cameron ran out of the store and across the parking lot to the adjacent gas station. The ensuing scene at the gas station involved Cameron trying to steal a car, blood everywhere, and a pair of handcuffs.

Before we hung up, Jon said "One round, hell, I would have fired every round in the gun!" That got me thinking, what would I have done in that situation? And that was the moment for me; right there, standing alone in the kitchen, just a few days before my 18th birthday. I realized that the world could go to shit in a heartbeat and I was ill prepared. I was cocky, untrained, and lucky. Suddenly, I didn't like any of those. Two months later, I was getting proper training under Jeff Cooper. So was Dan.

Jeff Cooper (left) congratulating Brad Ackman at the conclusion of his first handgun course at Gunsite.

RUSS SHOWERS

STARTING in the summer of 1982, I began my formal firearms training and it came very naturally. I was young, healthy, quick, had great eyesight, and most importantly, I was enthusiastic. I was the metaphorical sponge; eager to absorb the information and techniques, with no bad habits to get in the way and no physical injuries to limit me.

After a few years of training under Jeff Cooper, I wanted more. Competition was a nice addition, but really, I wanted to be an instructor. However, I was a 20-year-old newcomer hanging around in the company of 40 and 50-year-olds who had <u>serious</u> backgrounds. Becoming an instructor, shoulder-to-shoulder with these legends, was a long shot at best but I had nothing to lose. Jeff's Operations Manager was named Russ Showers and I asked Russ about the possibility of hiring me as an instructor. His reply: "Send me a resume." Damn it, that's not what I wanted to hear.

I had never needed a resume before because I was a college student and working summer jobs with landscaping or oilfield crews didn't require such a thing. What was I going to put on a resume? My name, address, and college GPA? Well, that's exactly what I did. It was pathetic, I knew it, and I was embarrassed to even send it. Russ called me a couple weeks later and told me very blandly that I was Gunsite's newest instructor, "Can you work the June 10th class?" So, that was my start as a firearms instructor, and I have Russ Showers to thank for it.

Brad Ackman (standing at left), Jeff Cooper (standing at right), and Russ Showers (kneeling). This image was taken in August 1983, just after Brad won the Man-on-Man competition during a handgun course at Gunsite.

COMBAT CHIROPRACTOR

It was in the summer of 1988 when I first met Ignatius Piazza. I was teaching a handgun course at Gunsite and he was there as a student. Everyone present in that course still remembers the scorn Jeff Cooper heaped upon Ignatius because he brought the "wrong" gun. On his name tape, Ignatius wrote the shortened, familiar version of his name, "Naish." Jeff had never seen such a name and therefore simply called this guy "Nash," the name tape be damned. That put me in a predicament, saying "Naish" to one and "Nash" to the other. The problem soon resolved. Jeff discovered that "Nash" was a chiropractor and took to calling him the "Combat Chiropractor."

Over the next few years, the Combat Chiropractor took numerous courses and gained quite a reputation as a serious, dedicated student. Naish and I were of similar age, skill, and enthusiasm so we soon became friends. Very early on in his training career, Naish had visions of opening his own firearms training school, and he was eager to show the world just how to do it.

In late-July of 1994, Naish took his dad and father-in-law to Alaska for a fishing excursion. I was living in Anchorage at the time and was naturally in charge of logistics for the trip. I had everything under control as much as possible, excluding the weather and the actual fish. As it turned out, we were treated to excellent doses of both. However, what most impressed Naish was my garage. That's right, my garage. It wasn't very big but it was perfectly organized, labeled, and clean. He genuinely liked that, and figured I might be the man with the organizational skills to serve as Operations Manager at the future Front Sight Firearms Training Institute. And so it was.

Naish Piazza (far right) is standing alongside father-in-law Irv Mueller (far left) and father Ignatius Piazza (center). Seward, Alaska, August 1994.

Okay, enough about me. The last few chapters served to outline my early years and set the stage. But really, this book is about all the interesting, ridiculous, and funny things which I have witnessed over the last 25 years. So, let the stories begin…in no particular order.

THE CLIENT

OVER the last 25 years, I have trained every imaginable sort of person. Dream up any combination you want of personality, background, and skill level and we have spent four days with that person. At every single course, we see a wide array of folks including:

- Average, everyday citizens who simply want to learn how to protect themselves and their families
- Hard-charging SWAT cops who are already pretty darn good upon arrival
- The proverbial "little ol' ladies" who are scared of the gun but even more scared of becoming a victim
- Business owners who are sick of being robbed
- "Soccer Moms" who spend too many hours home alone
- Competitors who come to tune-up their skills
- Military personnel of all stripes who are preparing for deployment, and
- Recreational shooters who bring a variety of guns because they are eager to try out their latest acquisitions

We see them all, and all are welcome at Front Sight. Our curriculum has something for everyone. If you are new and fearful of guns, we proceed at a comfortable pace and make sure that you fully understand all the equipment and terminology. If you are a seasoned shooter, we find whatever isn't yet perfect and make it so. If you are trying to better understand the intellectual and philosophical aspects of gunfighting, we make certain you fully absorb the classroom lectures. Below are a few examples of the wide variety of people who train at Front Sight.

Eddie was quite probably the best natural tactician I have ever seen. Good thing, since he was a member of the LAPD "D" Platoon which is essentially SWAT. Eddie moved with such stealth and ease through tactical simulators, I was actually jealous. He saw things that others missed and he identified targets at tremendous distances. When it came time to shoot, he was perfect. I once watched him deliver a flawless hostage rescue shot at maybe 15 yards, through a one-inch gap between a slightly open door and the frame. I don't know if his shooting was good enough to step up and pass the Handgun Combat Master Test, but it wouldn't surprise me. More importantly, if you call 911, this is the guy you want to show up. So, what could Eddie possibly learn from us? It wasn't easy, but I found something, two things actually. Eddie was as good as they get when functioning in a team environment with weapon in hand. However, I knew that even SWAT team members go home alone, with their handguns concealed under their shirts. And in that setting, he was less adept. So we worked on tactical movement as an individual and drawing his weapon from under concealment, and he definitely improved over four days. Eddie showed up already functioning at 95%. We worked diligently with him to eek out another percentage point or two. The curriculum has something for everyone, even accomplished shooters like Eddie.

I met Carla when she showed up to take a handgun course with us back in 2004. She was very much a lady and probably in her mid-30's. Even though it was June, she wore a long-sleeve turtle neck shirt and a pair of leather golf gloves. I assumed this was for sun protection but I later had a private conversation with her that explained everything. Her long-time boyfriend had gotten into drugs and completely lost his mind. He became hateful and abusive. She bailed out of the relationship, getting an apartment of her own across town. Ex-boyfriend tracked Carla down, got into her apartment, and hid in the closet, waiting patiently for her to come home. That evening as Carla stepped out of the shower, dirtbag stepped out of the closet, intent on raping and killing her. She was tiny compared to her attacker but she was determined to survive. During the fight, a large picture frame crashed to the floor and glass went everywhere. Dirtbag picked up a piece of that glass in his gloved hand and started hacking away at Carla. She was sliced to ribbons, including her hands, arms, and neck (thus the turtleneck and gloves). In the fray, she managed to pick up a piece of the glass, stick it into the leg of her attacker, and literally dive through the bathroom window. The neighbors intervened and dirtbag ran off. Carla knew it was only a matter of time until he returned. She was determined to never suffer that misery again. Carla was one of the most attentive students we have ever had at Front Sight. Her skills were middle-of-the-road, but her Combat Mindset was off the charts. Let Carla's story prompt others to get training before the mayhem starts.

David was in his mid-60's and lived in Orange County, California. He owned several very successful pawn shops and was a hands-on manager. He would personally assist the customers, take deposits to the bank, and close-up the store at night. During his first 28 years in business, everything was quiet and peaceful. David never even had a scare, let alone a robbery. He never felt the need for any protection greater than a telephone. Then in late-2009, some idiot stumbled into his store flashing a knife and making demands. David gave him a few $20 bills from the register drawer and everything ended peacefully. In early-2010, during the depths of the economic crunch, he was robbed twice in a single week. During the last robbery, David handed over the money but was shot twice anyway with a .22 handgun; once in the arm and once in the thigh. Enough was enough and David wanted out of the business altogether. However, selling his business in 2010 wasn't feasible, but a trip to Front Sight was. He took several courses from us using a variety of weapons. It was very entertaining watching him in the tactical simulators. He had some pretty strong, heart-felt words for the bad guys! David left us with a high level of skill and I have not heard from him since. I have no idea if he ever sold his business, but I am pretty sure the robberies stopped when he displayed a Front Sight target, shot completely to hell, in the front window of each of his stores.

Some of our students fight physical limitations such as severe arthritis, partial paralysis, missing fingers, missing limbs, a missing eye, or degenerative diseases. Of course, we are happy to train these folks, even if we need to modify our logistics or curriculum a bit to do it. Some years ago we trained a charming lady in her 30's by the name of Karen. Karen suffered from MS and when we first met her she used a walker. She took numerous courses from us so we got to know her well. Her energy level was such that she couldn't participate in 100% of the activities. Therefore, she focused on the skills needing the most work and sat out the stuff she was already good at. A few years later, Karen was confined to a wheelchair so we set up her chair with an appropriate holster and modified the techniques accordingly. Near the end of her training with us, she was only able to shoot a few relays in the morning, and a few more in the afternoon. Again, that was fine with us and we were happy to help however we could. Given Karen's very optimistic, compassionate personality, all the staff members were eager to work with her. Karen's gunfighting skills obviously deteriorated with her physical condition. What never waned was her interest and enthusiasm. She was always a warrior.

We train tens of thousands of students every year at Front Sight. The few examples above don't even come close to describing the wide variety of people we see. But, here is the punch line. Front Sight training is not about the weapons, or the facility, or the staff members, or the curriculum. It's about you.

FRIENDS IN HIGH PLACES

Bᴀᴄᴋ in 2006, we had a lady named Judy in a 4-Day Defensive Handgun course. She was perhaps in her late-40's and she absolutely loved the course. Over the four days, she mentioned repeatedly how she would like to get her 25-year-old daughter, Carly, out to Front Sight. At the conclusion of the course, Judy gave me a big hug and vowed that we would see her daughter soon.

A few months later, I got a call from Judy who told me her daughter Carly was enrolled to take the 4-Day Defensive Handgun course. Judy went on to tell me that Carly has had a rough time lately. She recently moved to California, was struggling to make ends meet, and was tangled up with an abusive boyfriend. I assured Judy that we would take good of Carly when she arrived.

I expected Carly to be a bit intimidated and introverted. Not even close. She was surly and resistant to the training. Carly was overflowing with comments like "Leave me alone, I know what I'm doing!" Before lunch on the very first day, she stormed off the range, crying, and went to sit in her truck and smoke a cigarette. I got a call over the radio from the Range Master who briefly described the situation. When I arrived, I asked the Range Master "Where is she now?" He gestured over to a full-size, dark blue, Dodge pickup...the one with the smoke billowing out of the window. I approached casually and said to her "I see things are not going very well. Can you tell me about it?" That was apparently the green light she was waiting for. She launched into a literal tirade of complaints:

- "You guys are such idiots."
- "You are treating me like a child."

- "I should be on a range by myself getting private instruction."
- "I have owned a gun for years and am better than all those other students."
- And on, and on, and on.

About this time Carly's cell phone rang. She answered it and I could hear a faint female voice on the other end which I recognized as her mother. Carly proceeded to say things like:
- "I can't stand these people."
- "I hate this place."
- "I should have never come."
- "Yes, mom, I took my meds."
- "No, you don't understand."
- "No, it's not going to get better."

She folded up the phone and tossed it onto the dashboard. I paused a few seconds and calmly asked if there was anything I could do to improve the situation for her. Based on her earlier comment, I even offered private training. She interrupted with "I'm telling Arnold!" I thought to myself "Who the hell is Arnold?" Maybe Arnold is her dad. Or her brother, or a friend. I had no idea so I asked "Arnold who?" She blasted me with "Arnold Schwarzenegger, you f***ing idiot! I am calling him right now. He WILL come out here, you know." At this point I was at the end of my rope and I mockingly said "If you call Arnold, I'm going to call George!" She dropped the transmission into drive and stomped on the gas. I stepped back a little bit but I neglected to notice this damn truck was a dually! As the truck ripped past me, the extended fender bumped me in the thigh and the rear tire just barely scuffed the very tip-toe of my boot. My foot got lucky, by about an inch! Those four spinning rear tires shot gravel all over me and the vehicles in the parking lot. She laid into the accelerator all the way out the front gate.

I'm pretty sure Carly lied to her mom about the meds.

CUPCAKE

FRONT Sight Alaska has a couple of nice lakes but no salmon streams. As such, we only see a few bears on our property each summer. In 2010, we were visited for a couple of weeks by a mother grizzly and her very young, very cute cub.

A bear's life in the summer is dominated by the quest for food. They emerge from hibernation hungry, so they eat. They need energy to cover lots of ground, so they eat. They want to enter hibernation in the fall as fat as possible, so they eat. Even so, our visiting cub took some time to smell the roses. He let mama provide the nourishment while he explored. You could tell exactly where junior had been by his tell-tale calling card. Junior was fond of standing up on his hind legs and touching things, as high as he could reach, with his right front paw. This stunt, almost like a "high-five," would leave behind a dainty, muddy paw print. The first such paw print I saw was on the front door of the house and it was not a perfect print, but rather a smear. The size and shape looked just like a cupcake, and from that point on, the cub was known to us as "Cupcake."

For the first week, Cupcake's antics were as cute as could be. He would leave his little paw print for us on the range chairs, the steel targets, and even the door of the truck. One night, Cupcake found that if he delivered his high-five to a paper target, his claws would dig in and the paper would rip off, resulting in a new play toy. Several nights in a row, Cupcake shredded every single paper target on the range, leaving behind a million gray and white scraps.

After cleaning up the range morning after morning, I remember saying "I wish Cupcake would leave us alone." And that was it, we never saw him again. Of course, everyone blamed me. The staff and students wanted to see more of Cupcake's paw prints and were livid that I had "run him off." I explained that I did no such thing, but they still looked at me as if I were Charles Manson or the like.

If you squint a little, and think sweet thoughts, this tiny bear cub footprint looks a bit like a cupcake with candles. Summer 2010.

DON'T FORGET YOUR RECEIPT

BACK in 2005, I got a call from a gentleman interested in a full-day of private training. I explained the cost was $1,000 for the day and we would provide whatever training he wanted. We could work with different guns, do some tactical exercises, and even dabble in ropes if he wished. "What would you like to do?" He said "I don't really care." "Well, okay, we'll figure that out when you arrive. I'll see you at 8:00 on Wednesday." He asked, "Can we make it 10:00?" "Certainly, it's your $1,000," I said.

Not knowing exactly what to expect, I had the Maintenance guys set up one handgun range, one rifle range, one simulator, and a zip line. The Pro Shop staff set aside a Glock 17, an Uzi, an M-16, and all the appropriate magazines and ammo. I obviously did not know exactly what the plan was, but I did not want to be the weak link and make our student wait while I got set up.

Mr. Private showed up at the prescribed time and I escorted him to the Pro Shop. I made all the appropriate introductions and had him sign the obligatory liability release. I had the Pro Shop staff run his credit card for the $1,000 charge and we were ready to get started. Now I actually <u>needed</u> to know what he wanted to do today. He asked if we could speak in private. We went just around the corner out of earshot of the staff. He said "I have everything I need and I'm going to head out." "What the hell? What do you mean?" I asked. He quietly explained that all he wanted was a receipt from "Front Sight Firearms Training Institute" which showed he was busy <u>all day</u>. That way, he could show his wife the receipt and she would have no suspicion that he spent the day at the brothels. I asked, "All you wanted was a $1,000 cover story?" He smiled and replied "Exactly."

I have had two more of these guys since. I kid you not. We even have a special name for them.

BUBBLICIOUS

IT was the third week of July in 2005 and the sockeyes were a little late getting into the Kenai River. We had caught a few but they were spread pretty thin. Gene and his wife Dianne asked me about taking them fishing the day after their Handgun Skill Builder course. I explained our recent lack of success and how it might be a long, fruitless day. Regardless, the weather forecast was for calm, sunny skies and they wanted to try.

We hooked the drift boat to my Suburban at around 7:00 a.m. and headed for the upper Kenai. We hadn't even left the driveway yet when Dianne asked me if I wanted some bubble gum. "Bubblicious, Strawberry-Kiwi," she said. "Uh, sounds really good, but no thanks," I replied. She wasn't deterred in the least and popped that little cube into her mouth. The interior of the vehicle soon smelled like a junior high school. An hour later, we pulled up to the boat launch and I was happy for the fresh air.

Sometimes rowing a drift boat is effortless. For example, if you are just floating with the current, from gravel bar to gravel bar, and getting out to fish, it couldn't be simpler. Or if you drop anchor in some likely-looking eddy, let go of the oars and pick up a flyrod, that too is pretty easy. However, what I was doing was hard work. I was rowing two plus-sized people, against the current, covering every inch of the river, for nine hours. I held the boat steady in the current so they could cast. I went round-and-round in every eddy giving them numerous chances at the fish. My shoulders were on fire and my lower back was screaming. Throughout the day, Dianne repeated her Bubblicious offer maybe a half dozen times. By now, I had come to associate my aching body and crappy attitude with the smell of Dianne's strawberry-kiwi gum.

I managed to get them into a few fish. They landed five and kept three, which was actually better than I expected. I took the obligatory photos, filleted the fish, and we headed home. Driving down the road I launched a preemptive strike against the stench of strawberry-kiwi and said "Boy, I'm a little warm. I hope this open window doesn't bother anyone."

At the conclusion of our day, Gene and Dianne didn't offer gas money, or reimbursement for the boat launch fee, or even a "Thank you." They simply walked away. After they departed, I cleaned out my vehicle. When I got to the back seat, I got a faint waft of strawberry-kiwi. Then I found it...a little memento from Dianne. Apparently on the drive home, Dianne had stuck a piece of well-chewed Bubblicious to the leather seat of my Suburban. That little pink blob taunted me. I was so damned mad that I actually took a picture of the chewed gum. My plan was to send Dianne the photo along with a scathing note, but I later thought better of it.

Gene and Dianne visited us in Alaska again the next year. I was a complete gentleman, taking the high road all the way. However, I had rehearsed an excuse in the event they asked to go fishing.

.505 GIBBS

FOR years, Jeff Cooper dreamed of holding a "Safari Prep" course. The curriculum would be based on his many African safaris and would be approximately 50% physical (shooting and gunhandling) and 50% intellectual (classroom discussions about traveling, logistics, selecting a professional hunter, etc.). I always wanted to participate in this course but Jeff refused to run it until he had a sufficient number of participants.

Well, in 2001 Jeff put out the word that he wanted to run the course and any interested parties should respond. Apparently he received a sufficient number of RSVP's and the course was on the books. Of course, I enrolled immediately to guarantee myself a spot. I was really excited to see a classroom full of the old guard, waxing enthusiastic about hunting the Dark Continent. There were nine of us.

Jeff had a small cadre of his favorite staff assisting in the course. Included in the staff was John Gannaway, a gunsmith and reloading technocrat from Phoenix. John's contribution to the curriculum was discussing which guns, calibers, and bullets are best suited for Africa. If the nuances between .458 Lott and .460 G&A, or pre-'64 Winchester and Dakota are your cup of tea, then John is your guy. These discussions were definitely my cup of tea and I enjoyed them completely.

Once everyone was thoroughly indoctrinated in the details of dangerous game rifles, it was time to shoot. John unveiled a dozen or so high-end rifles in a variety of calibers...all really big calibers. John gently displayed the rifles on a blanket which covered the tailgate of his truck. The smorgasbord included some gorgeous, traditional rifles with blued steel and walnut stocks as well as some modern fare in stainless and Kevlar. .375 H&H was the smallest cartridge represented and a couple of rifles starting with a "5" were the largest. I had shot .375 for years and wasn't going to waste my shoulder on that. Similarly, I had shot Jeff's personal .460 G&A many times over the years. However, I had never fired a .416 Rigby or anything that started with a 5.

The .416 Rigby kicked much harder than I expected; lots harder than a .375. I smiled at John and told him how nice that was. Next was the .505 Gibbs, but I must have showed a bit of hesitation. One of my classmates offered me a shoulder pad to dampen the recoil and maybe even minimize the bruising which was sure to follow. I liked the idea of a pad but when Jeff Cooper is watching, only a person of the lowest self-esteem would wear a shoulder pad. "No, thanks," I said. Shit, now I was committed. I figured the recoil and muzzle flip of this gun were going to be extreme, especially with a John Gannaway hand load stuffed into it. I had only two goals; don't drop the gun in the dirt, and don't let the recoil force me to take a step back (as that would be for sissies). So, I held on tight and leaned forward like never before. I was successful in both of my goals but I must say, one round of .505 Gibbs is plenty for a lifetime.

John hollered to the group "Next!" The next guy to line up behind the Gibbs proceeded to stand straight up, with a perfectly erect spine, and a gentle hold on the gun. This guy looked like he was shooting an air rifle in the Olympics. I leaned over to my shooting buddy and said "Watch this…he is going to get…" CRACK! In the blink of an eye the gun was pointed at the sky and the shooter had been driven 10-feet to the rear, stopping only because he thumped into the tailgate of John's truck.

Gannaway told the group "And that's why you lean forward."

900 YARDS OF B.S.

A friend of my daughter's from Riverton, Wyoming came to visit us in Las Vegas. His name was Zack and he was a small-town lad who had never ventured past Laramie or Rawlins or Cheyenne. Going all the way to Las Vegas was unheard of, and maybe even a little intimidating. As we sat around the dinner table one evening, Zack must have felt the need to impress. He proceeded to tell me some pretty heroic stories about his skills with a gun. One story involved him killing a running pronghorn antelope, with a perfect heart shot, 900 yards away, with an open-sighted .30-30 Winchester, while standing offhand. I thought about how ridiculous this tale was. However, I might be able to actually put his story to the test if I play my cards right. I responded with "Zack, have you ever shot an Uzi?" He said "An Uzi, hell no, I'd love that!"

Our guest was up early the next morning, excited by the prospect of shooting an Uzi. I too was up early to make sure I had my .30-30 and plenty of ammo. After the full-auto fun concluded, I introduced Zack to Sniper's Point, where we have targets out to 2,000 yards and beyond. I said "It's pretty fun to shoot at some of those steel targets WAY the hell out there. Wanna try?" I hauled out my .30-30 and presented it to him. I had him shoot a couple targets which were close in, roughly 100-200 yards away. Once he was warmed up, I asked if he could see the big white board with the letter "G" on it. He asked "No, where is it?" Pointing, I said "It's way out there, on that far ridgeline." Finally, Zack said "Oh yeah, I see it." "Good, good…try to hit the target just to the right of G." Zack spent the next 15 minutes doing his very best to lob a .30-30 bullet somewhere, anywhere, close to that target. We could easily see the puffs of dirt when the bullets hit the ground because the wind was nonexistent and sun was in our favor. In the end, he fired 42 rounds (all the ammunition I had brought), and the closest he came was maybe 10 yards away. Zack concluded "Man, that was impossible. How far is that target?" Feeling all warm and smug inside, I responded "900."

800 YARDS OF B.S.

My brother and I walked into a little roadside café in Kimball, Nebraska during the winter of 2010. We were drilling an oil well nearby and stopped in for breakfast before heading to the rig. As soon as we walked in, a grizzled old guy in the obligatory Carhartt jacket approached us and asked "Are you guys my hunters?" I told him that we were not his hunters but hunting sounded a good bit more interesting than what we had planned for the day. So, I invited the old dude to join us for breakfast while he waited for his clients. He told us he runs a bison hunting operation on a private ranch up near Scottsbluff. I asked all sorts of questions including the skill level of his average client. He snorted that most of his clients couldn't hit the broad side of a barn, from the inside. He recounted one client who wounded a bison at about 100 yards. The animal took off at full speed and the client completely missed several subsequent shots. "Carhartt Dude" was forced to shoot the animal before it vanished. Here are the details of his story:

- The rifle was a .338 Winchester Magnum with a fixed 4-power scope
- The bullet was 250-grain Nosler Partition (slightly heavier than the common .338 load and he was proud of it)
- The animal was at <u>800 yards</u> now, running at exactly 90°, left to right
- He stood up, fired one shot from offhand, and killed the bison instantly, with a heart shot, no less

"Wow, that's pretty impressive" I said, thinking this guy was completely full of crap. Sitting in a café in Kimball,

Nebraska was no place to call B.S. on Carhartt Dude. First, because I am a nice guy, but also because I had no testing grounds available to prove his story, one way or the other. But I could do the math and determine just what skill level this guy would need to make the hit. So, here are my assumptions and calculations. At 800 yards, the bullet would drop about 238 inches, or 19.8 feet! Flight time is about 1.22 seconds. A bison can run upwards of 35-40 mph. However, let's assume this particular animal was wounded and a little off his game. I'll give him a speed of 25 mph, which means he would run about 37 feet in one second. In 1.22 seconds the bison would cover about 44.7 feet. Now we know about the bison and the bullet. Let's see what the shooter had to do:

- Stand perfectly still while shooting offhand
- Hold the cross hairs exactly 19.8 feet above and 44.7 feet in front of the animal's heart and maintain those numbers while swinging the rifle to keep pace with the running animal
- Get a perfect trigger press so as not to upset the above calculations
- Hope there is absolutely no wind over the next 800 yards
- Hope the animal doesn't change direction or velocity
- Hope the bullet has enough energy left at 800 yards to kill the bison stone dead (as reported)

All I can say is I'm glad nobody was relying on <u>me</u> to make that shot in order to bring home dinner!

100 YARDS OF B.S.

BACK in 2005, I inherited a rifle from my grandfather. It was a pre-1964 Winchester Model 70 in .30-06. The old man had purchased it back in 1957, which was apparently a vintage year for that rifle. The gun had seen a modest amount of elk hunting in the Big Horn Mountains of Wyoming. The bluing was worn down to a nubbin in several spots from being carried in a scabbard, but the chamber and rifling looked pristine. I wanted to modify this gun a bit and then use it as my primary hunting rifle, replacing an old .270 I had used for years. Before I spent money on a new stock, scope, rings, etc., I wanted to see if this gun would shoot a respectable group.

I purchased four different factory loads to try. I knew if I could get a decent group from any of these factory loads, I could do even better with custom hand loads at a later date. However, if the rifle wouldn't group with any of this ammo, there might be an issue with the rifle itself. Trying to stack the odds in my favor, I waited until all the conditions were absolutely perfect (dead calm, overcast skies, a good night's sleep, and not too much Red Bull). I snuggled behind the rifle and slowly started shooting some groups at 100 yards. One of the four loads was completely useless, producing a group of maybe 3 inches. The other loads did better and produced groups of 1¼ to 1½ inches. Although a group of 1¼ inches would certainly suffice for hunting, I really lusted after a ½-inch rifle. I needed to know if the weak link in this deal was me or the rifle.

We had recently hired a new instructor to assist in teaching Precision Rifle. We anticipated great things from him because his resume described an impressive career as a Marine Sniper. He had apparently seen lots of action and made some pretty heroic shots. He happened to be on the property at that very moment and I figured if anyone can get the most out of this rifle, it's Dan. I honestly hoped he would shoot an itty-bitty ragged hole because then I would feel comfortable spending some money on this rifle.

"Sniper Dan" laid down behind the rifle and fired a group with each type of ammo. We went downrange to look at the hits and what I saw shocked me. The BEST group measured 5 inches! At first, I was disgusted. Then I realized he must have deliberately shot huge groups and was about to say something sarcastic like "I'll give you $50 for this worn-out piece-of-shit!" Instead, he was completely serious and thoroughly denigrated my rifle: "Won't shoot, won't ever shoot, no way." I simply thanked him for letting me tap into his vast skills.

I went ahead and worked on that rifle, fueled by a healthy dose of "I'll show you!" My efforts were pretty simple; a McMillan fiberglass stock, Talley bases and rings, a Leupold Mark 4 scope, and a good scrubbing with VFG pellets and Bore Bright. I tried a few more commercial loads and settled on a Federal Premium round with a 180-grain Barnes bullet. Twice I have shot ½-inch groups with that rifle. I saved one of those tiny groups and I stand ready to mail it to "Dan the Marine Sniper." I just need to figure out which McDonald's he is working at.

Brad Ackman with a respectable group from the .30-06 that "Won't ever shoot, no way." April 2006.

EVOLUTION OF INSTRUCTOR DEVELOPMENT

EVER wonder how Front Sight builds its instructor ranks? We do it through a process called Instructor Development, or "ID" for short. As you will see, there are many different approaches to ID in the firearms world.

Back in June of 1985, at the tender age of 21, I accepted Jeff Cooper's offer to become the youngest instructor in the history of Gunsite. Truth be told, it was Russ Showers who was willing to take a chance on me, not necessarily Jeff himself. Regardless, I was offered a position because of my shooting ability, not my resume. I had never formally instructed anyone in the use of firearms but I was damn sure excited about the opportunity.

I didn't have a clue what the training process would be for a new instructor. However, I knew it was going to be exhaustive, detailed, and state-of-the-art. After all, this instructor development process, whatever it was, had created the most celebrated cadre of firearms instructors in the world. How else did guys like Dennis Tueller, Greg Morrison, Robbie Barrkman, and Ed Stock get to be so good? This was going to be great!

My very first morning as a bona fide Gunsite staff member began with a hot breakfast cooked by Mrs. Janelle Cooper herself. Being an instructor definitely has its privileges! I was going to be working this week in a basic handgun course under Range Master Louis "Lewey" Awerbuck. Right after breakfast, Lewey told me to be at "The Barn" at 8:00 sharp to get the stuff we needed for the course. I knew the list included things like targets, tape, and spray paint. I was at least five minutes early to the barn because I wanted to earn my first brownie points. Lewey was already there and waiting for me. He bluntly guided me right past the targets and tape to a dim corner of the building. Once we were out of earshot of anyone else, Lewey spun around and looked up at me (he is quite short). He had a stern demeanor which very plainly said "I don't like you…not even a little." He distilled everything I needed to know about instructor development into one sentence: "You keep your f***ing mouth shut all week unless you ABSOLUTELY know what you are talking about." Wow, that's not at all what I expected but, of course, I said "Yes, sir." And that was my instructor development course at Gunsite.

The one-sentence approach to instructor development left a little to be desired. Clearly there had to be a better way. The next instructor development session I was associated with was more than a decade later. It was held at the miserable Global Security Complex south of Bakersfield. Front Sight was slated to open its doors to the public in a month's time and we needed to expand our staff roster. Naish retained a notable firearms instructor, let's call him "Mack," to run this Instructor Development course on our behalf. It was now Mack's opportunity to shine. We had gathered about 30 seemingly qualified guys from a variety of backgrounds including law enforcement, military, competition, and friends of friends. We had only two days to find their strengths, shore-up their weaknesses, and make sure they all understood, and could deliver, "the Front Sight way." A two-day stint was grossly insufficient unless the instructor candidates were 95% perfect upon arrival and just needed a little polish. The odds of that happening were about like the proverbial snowball.

Naish and I introduced ourselves to the group of candidates and quickly outlined the goals of the course. We wasted no time in handing it over to Mack because he had a shocking amount of material to cover in just two days. Mack introduced himself and then described some of the accomplishments he was most proud of in the firearms training industry. He also wanted the group to fully appreciate his prowess as an author and thus described the many articles and books he had written. To build credibility with the competitors in the bunch, he elaborated on his illustrious career of winning blue ribbons and gold trophies. Cautious not to waste a single minute, we ordered-in pizza from Domino's, which was the only pizza joint willing to make the arduous drive from Bakersfield. While we ate lukewarm pizza, Mack wanted everyone to know with absolutely certainty that he was the real deal in law enforcement circles. Mack told story after story and dropped name after name, proving beyond the shadow of a doubt that he was part of the inner sanctum at the Border Patrol, FBI, San Diego County Sheriff's Office, and even the Alaska State Troopers. Hell, he could show you the hats and T-shirts to prove it. To make certain that all spotlights were trained on him, Mack enthusiastically discredited every other trainer in the firearms industry. If you have heard of them, Mack slammed them. Jeff Cooper of "Scumsite" was an ego maniac of epic proportions, Masaad "The Boob" Ayoob was a raging alcoholic, and Clint Smith of Thunder Ranch was a small-time player intent on taking credit for the good work of others. And that rounded-out day one of the Instructor Development course.

That evening, Naish and I had dinner in a quiet corner booth at Denny's so we could commiserate and plan our next move. We whole-heartedly agreed that day one was a total loss. Mack needed some frank but friendly guidance on how to run a proper ID course.

Naish and I diplomatically took over the course on day two. We started the day with the instructor candidates shooting a brief skills test and then delivering some impromptu lecture blocks such as Three Secrets, Failure to Stop, and Presentation from the Holster. It was during these lecture blocks that I watched one of the candidates deliver the most compelling and professional lecture on Sight Alignment and Sight Picture I had ever seen…using props cut from yesterday's pizza box, no less. My spirits were lifted and I felt we may actually have a chance to produce some good instructors during that final day. Over lunch, Mack wanted the group to fully comprehend just how valuable he was to the Viet Nam war effort. Until mid-afternoon, Mack kept the group riveted with stories of crawling through the tangled underbrush with nothing but a K-Bar knife, defending the perimeter at night against hundreds of death-defying Viet Cong zombies, fording stagnant rivers teeming with leeches the size of beer cans, and becoming the youngest officer ever in the history of the Armed Forces. Amazing feats indeed, but we needed to wrap-up our Instructor Development course and figure out exactly whom to put in a gray and black uniforms. We stumbled through and managed to hire a few respectable instructors. Front Sight's first ID course was essentially a bust, but we got lucky the next month when there were only 10 students in our first course!

From late-1996 through about mid-1998, we took a different approach to instructor development. Succinctly put, it was the "Tag, you're it" method. If we needed additional staff on a given weekend, we would look over the roster of returning students and select the brightest stars. When they arrived at Sign In, Naish or I would pull them aside and say something like "We are very impressed with your progress…one thing that makes you a better shooter is teaching others…guess what, today is your lucky day…what size shirt do you wear?" I know it sounds unbelievable, but this approach actually worked pretty well. It worked because those long-time students were trained in our methods, could shoot very well, understood Front Sight's purpose, and were honored to be selected. Using this simple tactic, we landed a few guys who later became some of our premier Range Masters. Pat Lobb comes to mind, among others.

This system of selecting staff worked well but clearly had some flaws. The obvious disconnect here is "good shooter" does NOT equal "good instructor." And what about delivering lectures, running simulators, handling emergencies, etc.? Yes, we got lucky a few times with this approach but that was no reason to continue it.

Starting in late-1998, Naish created the next iteration of instructor development. For lack of a better term, this version could be dubbed "Mimic Me." Naish had a very "hands-on" approach to all aspects of Front Sight, so he actually ran the first couple of "Mimic Me" courses himself. Back in those days, we only ran one or two Instructor Development courses each year so enrollment was huge. We routinely saw 60 to 100 participants, all vying for a position as a Front Sight staff member. Naish assumed that some number of the participants would arrive fully trained and ready to wear the uniform. All we needed to do is locate them by means of a few basic drills and activities. Ah, the old "wheat from the chaff" trick. Surely, this couldn't take longer than a couple days.

After Sign In, we gathered all the participants in the white tent, which served as our classroom back then. You would expect the first discussion of the morning to be along the lines of:

- "Welcome to Front Sight, we're glad you are here."
- "You are going to learn lots and lots."
- "Our goal is to make you the best instructor possible over the next two days."
- "If you have any questions, don't be bashful, there are no stupid questions."

Wrong. Not even close. The room was silent and there was an uncomfortable tension in the air, just the way Naish wanted it. (There is no "boot-camp mentality" at Front Sight when it comes to training our students. Never has been and never will be. But when it comes to Instructor Development courses, we take a more regimented approach!) Naish stepped up in front of the group and gave the ID participants the tongue lashing of their lives. The discussion was overflowing with comments like:

- "If you are here just for a certificate, hit the bricks."
- "If you are here just for the money, hit the bricks."
- "If you are here just to build your resume so you can work somewhere else, hit the bricks."
- "We are going to take a five-minute break. If you came here for the wrong reason, don't be here when we start the next session. Simply hit the bricks."

When Naish first gave this lecture, it made even me cringe. This lecture/beating became legendary and it evolved into a badge of honor for those who survived it and actually got hired. To this day, some of the old timers proclaim "Modern ID is for pansies. Hell, I survived the Piazza gauntlet of fire. Now THAT was a proper ID."

For those who remained after the five-minute break, we headed out to the range to take the skills test we administer in the 4-Day Defensive Handgun course. This was the full test, complete with time pressure, concealment, reloads, and malfunctions. That probably sounds pretty basic to you, but remember, some of these people had never shot from concealment before or cleared a Type 3 malfunction. After tabulating the test results, we delivered the bad news. For those who finished down 80 points or more, it was time to "hit the bricks," and they did. However, before they departed, Naish graciously offered them a free 4-Day Defensive Handgun course so they could gain the skills they needed and return to another Instructor Development course better prepared. Many of them did just that and later joined our staff.

Those folks who survived the skills test were divided into groups of 4-6 participants. We very creatively labeled the groups A, B, C, etc. We gathered everyone into one large group and delivered a full lecture, such as Four Safety Rules, Type 1 Malfunction, or After Action Drills. Then we sent the participants to their respective corners to deliver that exact same lecture back to us...after having heard it only once. Now you see why I have dubbed this system "Mimic Me." Most people were very poor at this, which meant their demise. However, not everybody was a flop at this method. Long-time Front Sight students who had heard those lectures dozens of times were not intimidated in the least. Additionally, we saw a few actors and public speakers who were impressively proficient at memorizing a script. They stood up in front of the group and delivered their lecture in a smooth, comfortable, believable manner. They certainly handled a script well but don't ask them the difference between a revolver and a semi-auto!

"Mimic Me" was not true instructor "development" but rather instructor "try-outs." We didn't <u>develop</u> anyone in those four days, but we did find the 10% who had the potential to develop into great instructors. Of the folks we actually hired via this system, most still needed quite a bit of work to bring them up to the level of performance demanded by Front Sight. This was not the best arrangement because now they were on the payroll but they still needed true "Instructor Development." However, it was a better system than anything we had used before and was WAY better than anything being done elsewhere in the firearms industry.

At this point I had been exposed to four different styles of instructor development:
1. Shut your mouth
2. Listen to my stories…for two days
3. Tag, you're it, and
4. Mimic Me

None of the above systems were particularly successful unless the participant was highly accomplished upon arrival. What we needed was a system which would reliably recruit interested people and then <u>develop</u> them into quality instructors. Who ever said the participants needed to be at 95% upon arrival? Let's actually put some "develop" into instructor development.

In late-2000, Naish and I had a lengthy discussion about the goals of ID and how our current system wasn't delivering the results we wanted. At this same time, Naish was finding his days increasingly consumed by running and growing the corporation. I laid out my ideas for a new and improved course and he did the same. Together we arrived at a new approach and he gave me the reins to instructor development with the following mandates:

- Front Sight's ID course needs to be the envy of the industry
- ID participants must come to this course to earn a spot at Front Sight, not just build a resume
- Grow the staff sufficiently to keep pace with his marketing efforts (i.e. expect LOTS of students in the near future)
- Oh, by the way, you have about three weeks until the next ID course, so get cracking

I wanted to attract the greatest number of candidates possible and make my instructor development debut a resounding success. We cast a wide net by using the website, e-mail, snail mail, full-page newspaper advertisements, classified ads, lunchtime discussions during our courses, job fairs, and postings at nearby military bases. The phone and fax were soon working overtime and we were accumulating a nice group of candidates. Screening the candidates' qualifications was cursory at best. Basically, it was a "come one – come all" approach. I was never a big fan of filtering based on a resume because quality instructors like me would never have seen the light of day based solely on a resume. Similarly, I have seen untold dozens of hard-charging, dyed-in-the-wool, been-there-done-that warriors with stellar resumes who couldn't teach their way out of a wet paper bag. Resumes have been a poor predictor of the ability to teach others.

Before I could create the ID curriculum, I first had to define what it means to be a Front Sight instructor. This was harder than you might guess; much like defining one's Mission Statement. The quintessential Front Sight instructor is so much more than merely a good line coach and lecturer. We also need to be adept at safety, communication, customer service, troubleshooting, anticipating problems before they arise, and properly representing Front Sight even when off the range.

Now for the curriculum. First and foremost, ID needed to be four days long, not two. This I knew with absolute certainty. By late-2000, Front Sight was already steeped in the tradition of four-day courses and a four-day ID course would fit right in. Next, I created a set of exercises and lectures which I hoped would impart the greatest skill in the shortest time. At first there was no particular order to these exercises, more like a collection of loose puzzle pieces. The list of activities included:

- Shoot an introductory skills test with no concealment
- Shoot the standard first-morning demonstration
- Shoot each demo which accompanies lectures (Failure to Stop, Multiple Targets, Three Ways to Speed Up, Photographic Targets, etc.)
- Shoot a final skills test for score
- Deliver a self introduction
- Deliver scripted technical lectures in front of the group

- Coach students on the firing line
- Coach students in the simulators
- Understand intellectual and philosophical topics like different styles of learning, customer satisfaction, Front Sight's goals, etc.
- Interview one-on-one with a senior staff member

Placing the above tasks in the correct order was a definite chicken-and-egg problem. One could argue that lectures should come before shooting so the ID candidates had some philosophical understanding of what we expected. You could also argue that shooting should be first because if a candidate was absolutely dangerous with his weapon, why bother talking philosophy. We overcame the chicken-and-egg dilemma by giving the candidates a crack at multiple activities before even considering sending someone home. This way, no single bad performance meant the end of the line. By the end of the first day, we had seen a little bit of shooting, coaching, lecturing, and attitude. If most of these categories showed some promise, then the candidate continued. If most of these categories were hopeless, then a "goodbye" was in order.

Strange as it sounds, we also needed to define what it meant to "pass" ID and what it meant to "fail." It would be easy to proclaim "We are Front Sight! Nothing less than perfection will do. To pass you must shoot 100% on every test, every time. You must be able to deliver every lecture, whether in the classroom or on the range. You must be able to diagnose every shooting problem and have a dozen different tools to fix it." Rubbish. The best we can do is hire based on potential. We want to see if a candidate has a solid grasp of the fundamentals. If so, they "pass" and receive a uniform. We add sophistication and depth of knowledge with each passing course and each new student.

The instructor development process at Front Sight has evolved from a complete joke in the beginning under "Mack" to the very impressive program it is today. We now run ID courses every month of the year and our "passing" rate is generally about

30%. The ID process continues even <u>after</u> being hired. For example, during our regular courses when the students are in the classroom lectures, we gather the staff for some additional training and briefings we call Ongoing Instructor Development. Additionally, we run specific ID courses for those aspiring to move up from instructor to Range Master.

Even today, I continue to massage the ID curriculum and Naish continues to drive more and more instructor candidates into the course. Creating an instructor development program which is the envy of the industry has been tons of work, but I have never been one to "keep my f***ing mouth shut!"

Brad Ackman, looking serious, May 2012.

PIT CREW

GENERALLY, the biggest B.S. offenders are riflemen, but not always. We occasionally get calls from seasoned handgunners, usually competitors, who want to take the Handgun Combat Master test. They don't want to waste four days with unnecessary practice, mind you, they just want to shoot the test. Naish's offer is always the same; take the course from start to finish and if you pass the test, there is no charge. If you don't pass the test, you pay the full tuition. This gauntlet is enough to filter out all but the most confident. Over the years, we have had several people accept Naish's offer, and we were happy to deposit their checks.

One of the most memorable of would-be Masters was a guy from Austria who was a member of Team Glock. He was definitely an accomplished competitor and he was absolutely certain he would be the next Front Sight Handgun Combat Master. He accepted Naish's offer.

At Front Sight we are accustomed to students wearing jeans, T-shirts, and baseball caps. In stark contrast, this guy showed up in a silky, iridescent sweat suit with racing stripes. He carried a full suite of matching range bags which advertised "Glock" in silver embroidery. His gun was a custom Glock, obviously. The base plates of his magazines were even engraved with his initials and then plated in a brilliant, highly-polished chrome. He would have fit nicely into the Macy's Thanksgiving Day Parade. But, here is the crown jewel of his accessories - he brought along a lady to serve as his personal assistant! We took to calling her "Subservia," but obviously not in her presence. Every time the students gathered under the shade for a lecture, Subservia would ask the Range Master in her broken English how long this break would be. If this was a short break of just a few minutes, she would open a cold bottle of Gatorade and pour in a small envelope of white powder. She swirled the bottle until the magic powder was dissolved and then gave "Glitter Man" a few swigs. Then she moved over to his support side and deftly swapped the depleted magazines with fresh ones. She operated in complete silence so Glitter Man could listen to the lecture. This was clearly not her first time in the role of Subservia. This entire process was well orchestrated and fast, much like a NASCAR pit crew.

If the break was of greater length, then in addition to the magic Gatorade and fresh magazines, Glitter Man got his head wiped down with a damp terrycloth towel embroidered with the Glock logo. However, the damp-cloth routine removed all the sunscreen from his face. No problem; she quickly broke out a bottle of fancy European sunscreen and gently applied a fresh layer to his face. She was even in charge of placing the Glock baseball cap back on his head.

If the break was going to be a long one, she really had her work cut out for her. In addition to all of the above, Glitter Man got a massage. Yes…a massage. Every inch of Glitter Man from the waist up was coated in oil and rubbed vigorously. This was one hell of a sight. She worked his shoulders, arms, hands, and even his trigger finger. Once the massage was complete, she broke out some sort of chamois cloth and wiped off all the oil. Then came the obligatory Gatorade, magazines, and sunscreen. Subservia was busy even when Glitter Man was up on the firing line. This was her only opportunity to load magazines and stage all the supplies she would need during the next break. This business went on for <u>four days</u>. I don't know if she had duties in the evening as well.

This guy was clearly the Master, but not in the sense of "Handgun Combat Master." He finished the test in the middle of the pack, nowhere near the Master designation. His shooting was unremarkable, but everything else about him will stick with me forever.

THE PHILOSOPHY OF MASHING

We've all seen it. A shooter squeezes his entire hand, pushing the muzzle down, just before the shot breaks. At best, that shot will clip the very bottom edge of the target. Worse, it might skip off the gravel half way down range. This is called "mashing" and we can all agree it's not good.

The sequence of events in firing a handgun is essentially:
1. Point at the bad guy
2. Press the trigger which results in a bang, recoil, and muzzle flip
3. Push the gun back down to once again point at the bad guy
4. Repeat as necessary

A "mash" is nothing more than transposing numbers 2 and 3 in the above list. It simply means the effort to recover from recoil and muzzle flip came just a hair too soon. There is nothing wrong with pushing against the recoil. In fact, you <u>must</u> push, otherwise your gun remains pointed at the sky. The trick is to time the push properly. Jeff Cooper always divided timing of the push into two camps; "pre-ignition push" (before the shot is fired) and "post-ignition push" (after the shot is fired). Clearly pre-ignition push would result in a mash. Post-ignition push would result in a good hit and then get the weapon back on target. However, I believe there is a third option. How about "simultaneous-ignition push?"

Simultaneous means you push at EXACTLY the same time as the recoil and muzzle flip occur. "Simultaneous-ignition push" is largely a philosophical end point since it is almost impossible to time the push with such precision. Even trickier would be to apply the perfect <u>amount</u> of push, at the specific time, to exactly negate the effects of recoil and muzzle flip. Under these ideal and elusive circumstances, you would maintain a perfect sight picture through recoil. The slide would run back and forth as if the weapon were anchored in a vice.

Very few shooters have ever experienced a simultaneous, perfectly-metered dose of "push" using a fighting handgun. (It is obviously a good bit easier with a .22 than with a .45.) To perfectly fight recoil takes an incredible degree of muscle memory which comes only from firing thousands of rounds of identical ammunition through the same gun. For a period of about three years when I was competing seriously, I was occasionally able to maintain a proper sight picture during recoil. It certainly didn't happen with every shot, but maybe 25% of the time. Hitting a tennis ball or golf ball in the "sweet spot" is <u>nothing</u> compared to the satisfaction of watching the sights NOT MOVE during recoil!

Striving to achieve a simultaneous push has some merit in competition, but is not a worthy goal in defensive handgunning. Reason being, "simultaneous" is way too close to "pre" and you run the serious risk of mashing. Far better to allow the recoil and muzzle flip to occur and then immediately fix it. This can be done in perhaps 0.3 seconds. Saving 0.3 seconds on the street is not worth the risk of mashing a shot meant for the brain of the bad guy and instead hitting a loved one. Don't get too clever when lives are at stake. Be satisfied with "post-ignition push."

AND IN THIS CORNER

JOSH Gallager was 13 years old and far more interested in video games and cell phones than going to Alaska with his dad and sister. What could Front Sight Alaska offer anyway? Shoot some guns? "I can do that in Nevada." Chase salmon around in the Kenai River? "I hate fish and I hate fishing." Four days at Front Sight Alaska and there won't even be decent cell phone reception. Needless to say, Josh did not want to be there.

Josh and his dad, Ben, were pretty sassy with each other from the moment they arrived and, as far as I could tell, never saw eye-to-eye. Becca, the daughter, was at the other end of the spectrum. She was happy-go-lucky, comfortable around everyone, and clearly served as the buffer between young testosterone and old, rigid ways. She was only 11 but was wise and capable well beyond her years.

The very first day of their four-day stint started with a bit of a ruckus. The Gallager family had just pulled onto the property and stepped out of the car. Josh and Ben were already hollering at each other and it wasn't even 8:00 a.m. How bad could things be at such an early hour? Well, as I found out later, Ben had done absolutely no preparation for the trip. They had no rental car, no hotel rooms, and no real plan. Late-July at Anchorage International Airport is no time to be scrounging for a rental car. Late-July in Kenai is no time to be wandering hotel-to-hotel looking for vacancies. Out of options, the Gallager's bought a tent at the grocery store and pitched it in the trees adjacent to the baseball field...right there on Main Street in Kenai. "Welcome to Alaska kids! Never mind the mosquitoes. Need to use the bathroom? Go over there in the trees but don't let the passing cars see you. When you're all done, we'll go back to the grocery store and buy something for breakfast. Ain't life grand?"

Hell, I'd be mad too. However, I don't know if I'd be mad enough, like Josh, to punch my old man right in the eye in front of the Front Sight Alaska staff. Ben was knocked straight to the ground but Josh didn't rush in for the kill, thank God. Ben jumped up, embarrassed, and got in his son's face wagging a finger and spitting while yelling a reprimand. I thought to myself "Boy, I can't wait to put guns in their hands!"

Day three was to be spent floating the upper Kenai River in pursuit of rainbow trout, sockeye salmon, and great scenery. Before we departed for the river, I asked the entire family if they had the three things I asked them to bring; food, a fishing license, and a rain jacket. All three confirmed. I realized later that I had screwed this up. I should have said "Let me see your lunches. Let me see your licenses. Let me see your rain jackets."

We launched the drift boat at Sportsman's which is a popular spot on the upper Kenai. Everything was seemingly perfect. The sun was shining. The fish were splashing. The Gallager's weren't fighting. We got maybe an hour into the float when the clear blue sky was eclipsed by heavy black clouds. This change happened very quickly, within just a couple of minutes, and we were clearly in for a significant thunder storm. I dropped anchor and put on my rain jacket. The first couple drops were already hitting around us and I advised my fellow fishermen to put on those rain jackets. I got blank stares from all three. "We don't have any jackets." What the hell? We went over this already. What happened next I am not proud of, but I would do it again.

I keep my boat in immaculate condition and stuffed full of anything, everything, that might be needed on the water. I had enough rain jackets for our entire crew and three more just like it. However, I told them "I only have one more rain jacket…size Small…which will fit Becca perfectly. Father and son, you guys are screwed." The clouds soon opened up in earnest. Becca and I were fat and happy, completely dry inside our rain jackets. At first, father and son acted as if the cold rain was no bother. "We're in Alaska, man…what's a little rain?" In just a few minutes, the bravado gave way to bitching. "Josh, I told you to pack the rain jackets." The complaining soon gave way to pleading. "Brad, do you think we could just row downstream to the take out?"

It was satisfying to allow nature to punish these two fools. Act like idiots and get into a fist fight at Front Sight, there will be some sort of retribution. Ah, Karma.

A glimpse of the torrential thunder storm that brought an end to our fishing trip and a smile to my face. Summer 2008.

DON'T CROSS THE STREAMS

EVERYONE remembers the movie *Ghostbusters*. If not, go get reacquainted! Recall the important safety tip for using the particle accelerators; "Don't cross the streams...it would be bad...try to imagine all life as you know it stopping instantaneously." Universal Firearms Safety Rules 2 and 3 are just like that. You cannot, you must not, violate both of these rules at the same time. You might get away with covering yourself or someone else with the muzzle if your trigger finger is straight. You might get away with putting your finger on the trigger if the muzzle is in a safe direction. Make both of these mistakes at the same time and there is hell to pay.

Back in the '80's I had a high school friend named Daniel who was an avid hunter. That particular year he drew an elk tag for a coveted, very-restrictive area in northwestern Colorado. Daniel and his dad had applied for those tags year after year and were finally successful. Father and son had done a modest amount of scouting before the season. Several times they had seen good-sized bulls on a particular ridgeline just as the sun was coming up. This seemed like the obvious place to hunt come opening morning. As a bonus, their campsite would be a picture-perfect spot in the valley adjacent to a creek, just a short trek from the ridgeline.

Crawling out of a down-filled sleeping bag on a cold November morning is always easier said than done. But in short order, the backpacks were on, the headlamps were illuminating the way, and father and son were hiking up the mountain with enthusiasm. Dad was in the lead and Daniel was a few steps behind. Daniel was carrying the brand-new rifle his dad had purchased for him shortly before the season. It was a 7mm Remington Magnum which is certainly an excellent choice for big elk. Daniel wanted to be ready for anything, so he chambered a round while still in camp and then slid the safety off. Daniel had his finger on the trigger as he followed his dad's footsteps up the hill. The muzzle was pointed generally up and forward because that was the most comfortable position for Daniel while hiking.

Daniel's foot slipped just a little in the loose rock and he stumbled to his knees. The butt of the rifle hit the ground. Daniel's ears were ringing and he wondered "What the hell was that noise?"

The bullet hit dad in the base of the skull at an upward angle. This was a sight nobody should have to see, let alone a son. It took several hours for Daniel to muster the focus to drag his father down to camp and get help. Daniel was never the same, and dad simply was no more.

Seriously, don't "cross the streams."

TAP, TAP, SLAP

Back in 2000, I came to learn that the only people goofier than firearms instructors are martial arts instructors. Front Sight was preparing to launch our martial arts program and we wanted some outside influence. Sure, we had some martial artists on staff, but largely we were gun guys. For a full year, we conducted interviews and auditions to find the proper person to run the martial arts curriculum at Front Sight. We had no predetermined fighting style or curriculum; all we had was a completely open mind.

I placed ads in the Las Vegas newspaper and a couple of magazines. In addition, we sent a flyer to everyone on our mailing list. And the responses flooded in. I received so many responses that I couldn't even begin to keep up. I hired a full-time staff member just to sort through the resumes, letters, e-mails, phone calls, and DVDs. He built a huge spreadsheet of all the candidates and sorted them by fighting style. We wanted to audition all the candidates of a particular style at approximately the same time. In other words, we tried to audition all the Jiu-Jitsu guys one right after another. Then all the kickboxers, then the Muay Thai guys, then the mixed martial artists, etc. We slated four hours for each audition which consisted of an interview, some demonstrations, and then some actual teaching using selected Front Sight staff as students. If the candidate wanted more time, or more mock students, or some of his staff present, we were happy to accommodate. We video taped every audition so we could refer back with greater clarity.

The first two auditions went extremely well. These first two guys were true experts, great instructors, and well spoken. I had the feeling this audition thing was going to be easy. After the first two however, we suffered a rash of:

- Tattoos covering the hands, neck, and face
- Felony convictions
- Numerous prison sentences
- Guys who couldn't speak English
- Guys from foreign countries who lacked valid work visas
- Guys who wanted payment for the audition, and
- Guys who didn't even bother to show up

After a couple of months, our luck improved and we auditioned some good candidates once again. Most of the people we auditioned seemed to be solid instructors and capable fighters, but not all. We auditioned a gentleman from New Mexico who had sent us a DVD in advance. The video contained some pretty interesting stuff. He had blended his knowledge of human anatomy, specifically the nervous system, with his martial arts background to create a "new" style of fighting. The idea was to poke your opponent in a few specific places, in a specific order, and he would collapse into unconsciousness. I'm telling you the truth; that's what he said and that's what his DVD showed. Our candidate had dubbed his new technique "The Great Equalizer" because even a small woman could use it successfully against a big, drunk brute. Funny, I thought the term "Great Equalizer" was already taken and referred to your Glock! Regardless, "Mr. Nerve Poker" showed up at the designated time with four of his staff instructors. They interviewed well enough and then they led us through some stretching exercises and basic strikes. Then came the discussion we were all waiting for. Mr. Poker explained to us the anatomical reasons why you can deliver a couple of taps, and then a slap, and have your opponent pile up like a wet rag. Mr. Poker demonstrated the tap-tap-slap technique on one of his assistants, and I'll be damned, the guy fell down right in his tracks. Maybe 10 seconds later, the assistant came-to and went to the sidelines to fully recover. The obvious next step was to try this technique on us. Bill went first. Mr. Poker delivered the tap-tap-slap to Bill and not a bloody thing happened. I was disappointed because I really wanted to see Bill flop to the ground. Mr. Poker described that heart rate sometimes affects the results. "In a real fight, your heart would be racing and the results would be better." So, Bill began a strenuous series of jumping jacks and push ups. Mr. Poker delivered the tap-tap-slap again. Same result. I said "Try it on me." I did the obligatory exercises and then received the tap-tap-slap. Nothing. Then Mr. Poker tried it on Tim and Daryl. Nothing. Five minutes later we were shaking hands with Mr. Poker and bidding him farewell. Don't let the door tap-tap-slap you on the ass on the way out.

We auditioned a guy from northern California who claimed to be a Jiu-Jitsu practitioner. This guy was a bit odd and he constantly referred to choking his opponents. Every discussion and every technique ended with an opponent who had been choked-out. This guy seemed to me to be full of hot air. He didn't carry himself with confidence, certainly not like an accomplished fighter. He had no command presence in front of the group. His lectures were helter-skelter at best. Finally, I had enough. I called his bluff and said "I want you to choke me out." I figured the worst case would be the loss of a few brain cells. His eyes went wide at my request. I told him "I'm serious, so let's get to it." I gave him no choice so he stepped in behind me and applied a choke hold. He put the squeeze to my neck for maybe a minute before letting go. It was pretty uncomfortable; however I never even saw stars, let alone passed out. I said "Certainly a Jiu-Jitsu stud like yourself can choke somebody out. Try it again." He did, with the same result. At this point, I had my own Front Sight guys chomping at the bit to give it a try. I was too smart for that!

We auditioned a hard-style Karate guy from Las Vegas who was in his mid-40's, well built, and seemed like the real McCoy. He was very professional in his interview and conducted group activities quite well. There were seven of us and one of him, for a total of eight. At his direction, we divided into four groups of two. Due to the odd number of Front Sight staff, I was teamed up with him. The exercise at hand was to have one partner slowly throw a big, horizontal, "haymaker" punch. The opposing partner would duck under the punch while stepping in to deliver an elbow to the ribs. Since I was his partner, Mr. Karate demonstrated on me. Displaying no control whatsoever, he delivered an elbow to my ribs with such force that it folded me over like a taco. I couldn't even stand up, let alone stand up straight. Off to the emergency room I went to confirm a broken rib. Can't you just see this guy, breaking the ribs of our First Family Members? His audition was cut a bit short.

I got a call from a very successful business consultant in California who wanted to audition. I knew of this gentleman from his business activities but I didn't know he was a martial artist. Truth be told, his martial arts resume was pretty thin. He formerly owned a karate studio in downtown San Francisco but sold it years ago. This whole thing seemed strange to me. Here was a guy who was:

- In his late-40's
- Very wealthy
- Living in northern California which is a long commute from Front Sight
- Busy all the time delivering business seminars, and
- Hadn't been active in martial arts for years

Regardless, he wanted to audition to be our martial arts guru. Okay. He was so completely certain that he would be the best candidate that he wanted to audition last. He actually said to me "You've seen the rest, now prepare to see the best." I didn't think anyone actually talked like that. I thought that mantra was reserved for billboards advertising the "best cheeseburger in town." Well, there was no burger, but this guy was certainly cheesy.

As he requested, I scheduled him last. He arrived at Front Sight in a limousine with his wife and kids. He introduced himself to the group, which took over 15 minutes. Then he got us into a formal, straight line and guided us through some Kiddie Karate exercises. We all squatted down, square-on to our imaginary opponent, and threw choreographed punches into the air, crisply retracting the opposite arm directly under the armpit. I remember doing this exact same thing when I was eight years old at a YMCA day camp and I thought it was silly even back then. As with all the candidates, we had set aside four hours for his audition. About an hour into it, we took a break. As we sat and drank water, I asked him about his gun take-away techniques. He said he never really did those back in the early-'80's in San Fran. I said "Let me show you a very basic technique that I know and you can give us your opinion." He agreed. I was the mock victim and he was the bad guy. He walked up behind me and poked a red Glock between my shoulder blades. I spun around and forced the gun out of my back with a forearm-to-forearm block. Before I even had the chance to trap his arm and remove the gun he screamed "STOP!" He went on to reprimand me by saying "This is a training session, not a street fight. Why would you dare hit me so hard as to potentially cause a bruise?" Mr. Kiddie Karate's children were pretty young and still thought dad was cool. The wife knew better. She was grossly embarrassed by her husband's display of incompetence and childish outburst. She bowed out (literally) and went to sit in the limo. I gave Mr. Kiddie Karate another 30 minutes and then shook his hand…very gently.

In the end, I tapped into the talent we already had on staff. I selected two of our firearms instructors who also had years of martial arts experience to run the program for us. It took a year of searching, thousands of dollars in payroll, and one broken rib. What do you know…the best guys were right here the whole time.

Not Enough of a Good Thing

Alaska Industrial Hardware in Kenai caters to commercial fishermen in the Port of Kenai and the oilfields at nearby Swanson River. In 2004 when we were just setting up Front Sight Alaska, I needed all sorts of stuff including hardware and tools. While perusing the aisles of Alaska Industrial Hardware, I saw a screwdriver made specifically for Paul Bunyan. It was about four feet long with a shaft the size of a paper towel tube and a handle as big as a tennis ball can. What a joke, I thought, pushing a tool way beyond its intended application.

That's also how I feel about "pocket pistols," but obviously in the opposite direction regarding size. Take a perfectly functional, manageable weapon, place it in the magic shrinking machine, and out comes an uncomfortable, unreliable, unmanageable trinket which more resembles a stocking-stuffer than a proper handgun.

Now granted, I would much rather have a pocket pistol than a ball point pen if those were my only two choices. However, it is very easy these days to carry and conceal a proper handgun, regardless of who you are. Why bother with "Honey, I shrunk the handgun"?

When the "chips are down," do you really want the miniature version in your hands?

GHETTO GUN

A friend of mine named Rob MacLeod is fond of saying "There is no bad equipment, only the bad <u>use</u> of that equipment." Yet there must be an exception to every rule. The Cobray M-11 submachine gun is that exception. Other than price, the M-11 has no redeeming qualities.

To support the one-day submachine gun courses Front Sight was running back in 1999, we purchased 150 M-11 submachine guns, Model POS-A1. At the time, I was surprised how inexpensive and readily available they were. Little did I know. When the guns came in, I ran a staff development day so we could familiarize ourselves with this new system. We shot every single gun to verify that it functioned properly and was sighted in. At the end of the day, we had a large and growing pile of broken guns. This was clearly an omen.

Over the coming months, breakage came in many forms. By far the most common malady was the collapsible stock giving way under recoil. When it did, the gun flew backwards and the shooter received the full brunt of the rear sight directly into the safety glasses. We spent ridiculous sums of money on new safety glasses until we got smart. We welded a little button on the stock in just the right spot to keep the stock from collapsing. That fixed the problem but then we needed twice the amount of room inside the safes!

Another common problem was the "runaway gun." If the sear decided to malfunction, the gun would fire every single round in the magazine…even if your trigger finger was straight. There was no advance warning for this problem so we had to address the possibility in the morning lectures. Some students secretly hoped they would get a runaway gun so they could shoot more ammo! From the perspective of the staff, the runaway gun was a hairy situation.

The muzzle was not the only place on the M-11 that would launch dangerous projectiles. The checkered bolt knob on top of the gun would routinely shear in half and fly off. We kept big Ziploc bags of them as spares on each range. They were stored right next to the Band Aids because if you needed a new bolt knob, you also needed a Band Aid for your forehead.

The ejection port was the second scariest hole on the gun. It would spit brass so violently that we had to plan for it. If we had a shooter who was timid, we placed them on the far left side of the line to reduce the number of things that would hit them. They might still get a bolt knob to the face, but they wouldn't get pelted by their neighbor's brass. I long wanted to set up a chronograph to measure the velocity of the flying brass, but I never did. I know the velocity was shockingly high because I saw its effects many times. On one notable occasion, Instructor Doug Oliver was talking to a lady from her right side…the ejection port side. While Doug was explaining a technique, she pressed the trigger. The brass hit Doug in the mouth so hard, it knocked a front tooth clean out of his head. I kid you not; he spit out both the hot brass and the displaced tooth.

Breakage was so rampant that we had a formula for it. For a relay of 20 shooters, we brought out 40 guns. That was the formula; bring out 200% of the guns you think you will need.

Using a naked M-11, without a suppressor, was a dubious situation for the support hand. By adding a suppressor, the muzzle was extended much farther forward which helped protect the support hand from getting perforated. Therefore, we equipped each gun with a suppressor made by Coastal, Model POS-A2. This particular suppressor was neither well made nor very quiet, but it sure was heavy! And the damn thing got extremely hot after just a few shots. So much so, we had to make little insulated sleeves, like oven mitts, for each one. This helped prevent seared skin, but keeping the oven mitt in place was almost impossible. Hell, keeping the entire suppressor on the gun was tough! The suppressors loosened just a little bit with each shot. After a couple hundred rounds, they were sloppy loose. Early in the program, we had several suppressors fall right off the gun and land at the feet of the shooter. Other suppressors managed to stay on the gun but were hanging at an angle when the next rounds were fired! It was pretty exciting when the target got peppered by chunks of bullet, chunks of suppressor, and chunks of carbon, all at the same time. To stop this silliness, we modified the curriculum. Tightening the suppressor became part of the After Action Drills:

1. Quick Check
2. Final Check
3. Scan
4. Tighten that heavy, fat, white-hot, overpriced pipe that is protruding from the front of your gun

And the magazines! The factory Cobray magazines, Model POS-A3, were little more than 9mm Pez dispensers. The thin plastic feed lips wore down so quickly and so thoroughly that you never knew just how many rounds would be set free at any given time. The soft plastic body would bulge so badly that it wouldn't fit in the gun (but it always fit in the trash can).

Once in a great while we got students who were familiar with subguns and they would comment "Man, these M-11's are crap!" "Yes, yes" I would say, "but we're providing free pizza at the end of the day!" Naish would follow with "And where else are you going to get a free one-day submachine gun course?" He was right. Those miserable M-11's and the thousands of people who attended those free subgun courses put Front Sight on the map.

After the shooting came the cleaning...and we got pretty good at the cleaning. We learned early-on that a production-line approach was best. The first station was disassembly. Then came cleaning, broken parts replacement, lubrication, and finally, reassembly. A dozen guys could make it through 50 or so dirty

M-11's in an hour. In an effort to save time, I once tried an ultrasonic cleaner. I had never before used this gizmo and it looked just like a stainless steel deep fryer. I mixed up a solution of Simple Green, placed several types of guns inside, and hit the "ON" button. An hour later I opened the lid. The Glock was perfect, no surprise. The revolvers looked good too. But the M-11 was silver. It went in black, and came out silver! There was exactly zero bluing left on the gun. Only an M-11.

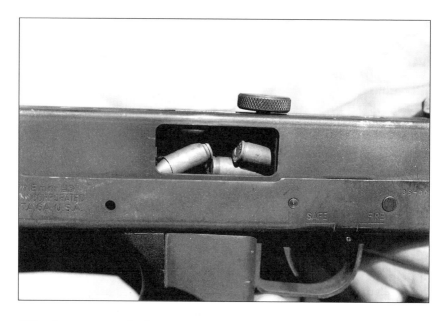

What's wrong with this picture? This was the typical malfunction when too many rounds were set free out of the magazine. November 1999.

Cleaning the suppressors was another issue altogether. After a day of shooting, those Coastal suppressors were so caked with carbon that we could hardly get them apart. The normal disassembly method was to remove the threaded end cap and then pour out all the baffles which looked like regular fender washers from Home Depot. We could generally remove the threaded end cap by using a padded vice and a pipe wrench. Getting the "fender washers" out was virtually impossible. We tried beating on them. We tried heating the whole thing with a propane torch. We even tried sandblasting them free. Nothing worked consistently until one of our guys, the pyromaniac in the group, made a suggestion. "What if we fill the suppressor with propane, ignite it, and blow all the parts out the open end?" I'll be damned, this actually worked. However, you need to launch the washers into some sort of backstop or you will spend hours looking for parts, much like an Easter egg hunt.

Part of our free submachine gun course was a demonstration put on by Naish. In this demo, he would shoot a few targets with the M-11 until it was empty, drop it to the ground, and continue with his Glock 22. The students would comment "Wow, that was a great demo!" What they didn't know was the satisfaction Naish received from throwing that M-11 into the dirt. He would have thrown it to the ground even if nobody was watching!

You know the old saying about sailboats; the two happiest days are buying and selling. With the M-11, there is only one happy day...buying (and that is due strictly to ignorance). Come to find out, there is no happiness in selling M-11's. We graduated from M-11's to Uzi's in late-2000 and Naish asked me to sell off the M-11's. It seems the M-11 is the only full-auto weapon which actually loses value with age. You could send your kids to college by investing in MP-5's or M-16's. But the M-11 is like buying a brand-new, overpriced car; it's all down hill from here.

Brad Ackman lecturing with the M-11 submachine gun.

THE OL' SNIFF TEST

AT Front Sight, we are quite serious about the safety and security of our students. As part of that effort, we run criminal background checks every year, on staff and students alike. The fact that someone had a clean background <u>last</u> year is marginally interesting <u>this</u> year. We also request a "Character Witness Statement" which gives us additional comfort. The overwhelming majority of our prospective students enjoy a spotless background. They welcome a background check and have no trouble finding a friend or colleague to submit a character witness statement.

Simply passing the criminal background check does not guarantee a person will get training at Front Sight. Everyone is still subject to "the ol' sniff test" once they arrive. We at Front Sight are an open-minded group of people and we are happy that so much diversity exists in our student population. We certainly don't limit training only to people who look, or act, or think a certain way. However, if someone arrives at Front Sight who looks or behaves in a suspicious manner, we intervene immediately. The approach is always the same; we engage them in a direct, candid conversation. Let me give you a couple of examples.

In June of 2007, we had a young man swagger up to the Sign In table for his 4-Day Defensive Handgun course. He was dressed in baggy jeans, a sloppy oversized T-shirt, and a baseball cap which was perched sideways on his head. Tattoos covered probably 80% of the skin I could see, including a good portion of his face. He was alone and was renting one of our Glock 17's. I looked at the roster and found that he was 19 years old. I'm no expert, but this kid looked like a gang member. I asked the opinion of a couple other staff members who had dealt with gangs extensively in their law enforcement careers. "Yep, looks like a gang banger." I politely asked this guy to step over to the side for a quick chat. I said "Please take no offense, but with your clothing, your tattoos, and your swagger, you look like a gang member. Are you?" He smiled and said with pride "Hell yes!" He went on to explain that he lives in a tough neighborhood in L.A. and he wanted the best training possible. I thanked him for his candor and then apologized that Front Sight wasn't the place for him. We shook hands and he departed like a complete gentleman.

Maybe six months after the above story, it seemed to be happening again. This time the student was a little older, maybe early-30's, and he was scheduled to take a rifle course. I pulled him aside for the obligatory chat…"Please take no offense, but with your clothing, your tattoos, and your swagger, you look like a gang member. Are you?" He laughed. "Hell no, I'm a DEA agent and a Diamond First Family Member." He proudly whipped out his badge to dispel any doubt. All I could say was "I bet you get lots of undercover assignments."

In early-2000, during our relentless delivery of the free subgun courses, we saw folks from all walks of life. And we saw them every day. It took a real character to stand out from that crowd, and a few did. On this particular morning, I was standing just outside the classroom greeting the arriving students as they walked over from the parking lot. I noticed a ratty-looking white Ford van pull into the parking lot. It had no windows in the cargo area and bumper stickers seemingly everywhere. The driver put the van in park and turned off the engine but didn't get out for quite some time, maybe 10 minutes. Eventually, a short, middle-aged man stepped out and went to the back of the van. He opened one of the panel doors, reached inside, and came out with a guitar case. He quickly closed and locked the door, as if to prevent anyone from seeing the contents inside. He stood like a statue at the back bumper for another couple of minutes. This was already strange, but was about to get more so. As if mustering his courage, the man looked nervously over both shoulders and then walked very slowly in our direction. All I could imagine was this guy pulling a Tommy gun out of that guitar case to commit suicide-by-Front-Sight-instructor! Thankfully, that was not to be. He stepped up to the Sign In table and I casually said "Good morning." He was courteous and replied with the same. I asked him the obvious question; "What's in the guitar case?" He simply replied "A guitar." Hmm, that's not actually what I expected. I said, "There won't be an opportunity today for you to play the guitar, so I recommend you leave it in your van." He said that he couldn't do that. When I asked why, he said "Because they will de-tune it." I asked, "Who will de-tune it?" He looked to the sky and in a hushed tone said "You know…them." I said, "But if it's locked in your van, THEY won't be able to get to it." He rebutted, "THEY are everywhere. The van won't stop them. The only place my guitar will be safe is in my hands." Holy shit, I thought I was on an episode of Candid Camera. With great aplomb, and $20 for gas, Naish sent this gentleman back home. We just couldn't be responsible for an alien guitar de-tuning. Not today.

Sometimes, the ol' sniff test is actually a sniff test. We have had a handful of students over the years stay up late, drinking with their buddies, the night before a course. Come 8:00 a.m. they are still reeking of alcohol and we pull them aside for the big chat. To date, each and every one of these drinkers was a guy; not once was a lady. Almost every one of these guys was thrilled to be called out and sent home. They were either exhausted or sick, or both. The notion of standing in the sun all day, trying to pay attention, with all that noisy gunfire, was just too much. Their dismissal from the course was exactly what they wanted exclaiming "Now I can go back to the hotel and sleep."

Sometimes, the ol' sniff test comes in the mail. Not long ago, I received a hand-written letter from a prospective student. It was on dime-store stationery and seemed to be written by an older man. I found it so odd, so peculiar, that I have included it here. Except for his personal data, I have retyped it to exactly match the original, complete with all the syntax errors, omissions, and misspelled words. I support this fellow's desire for training; it just won't be here at Front Sight.

02-28-2011
Front Sight Pro Shop
Front Sight Road
Pahrump   N.V. 89048
5:00 PM

Sir: Today at 2:00 PmE.S.T. A man yelled out Loud you better Run Old man .as Fast and far as possible.

One Year ago May 2010 My wife and I moved To This lovely complex. In June of 2010 I started taking Pictures with my 35 MM Camera of Wild anmials and InsecTs. You see Iam 100% disability retired from work due To physical limations. I use To enjoy taking pictures. I did noT Know My Flash on the camra would cause The young people To sTarT ~~folling~~ following me around To vo<u>n</u> and on my trip back To Calif To bury a Korean War vet IN Dec 2010. 2 Sunday's ago I tried To go To Church and worship The Lord. a white van pulled in Front and Impared me from going To Church. Well Sir To This day My My wife and I never bother any one Here at Complex.

I meet with my Pastor and told Him of the Sunday Imper-ment To me. Now law inforce ment patrol complex very Heavy. Iam oN a Fixed Limmited Income, Never held firearm in my Hand. I am Fearfull for my Wife and my self. We do noT know what Todo since that Thug said You better run. Old man. WhaT can I do To stop them with God's Help and Your Trainning? I am Willing To show Proof of Income for a possible discounT course.

God Bless,

Mr XXXXX

PS: <u>I am afraid To go To DocTor my wife does noT know To much</u>

As you know, part of our Mission at Front Sight is to reach the 95% of the gun owning public who need training. Those who fail the ol' sniff test we affectionately refer to as "The 96th Percentile;" those people who we wish we had never reached!

BECAUSE THEY DON'T MAKE A .46

THE initial volley in the great handgun caliber debate is usually something like:

"Why do you carry a .45?"

"Because they don't make a .46."

Okay, we get it…bigger is better. I too prefer .45 over .40, and .40 over 9. However, the discussion of terminal ballistics (actually stopping bad guys) is so much broader than just caliber.

The real key to success is delivering hits to the proper spot, quickly. This means you must be able to actually shoot the gun. Now we are talking about sights, trigger, fit in your hand, etc. It also means the gun must go "bang" every time. Now we are talking about reliability, magazines, and proper ammunition. It also means you must have the gun available when you need it. Now we are talking about proper size, reasonable weight, dehorning, holsters, and concealment garments.

Given a choice of full-size handguns, all with proper sights, triggers, and reliability, I would choose .45 over the other calibers. However, given a choice between a full-size, properly-equipped Glock 9mm and a rinky-dink Derringer .45…

To sit around and ponder calibers and terminal ballistics to the exclusion of all other factors is the domain of theoretical physicists, lackey gun writers, and the unenlightened. Yes, caliber matters. But caliber is not the most important consideration. YOU are the most important consideration. Your ability to get hits, quickly, and under stress, will determine the outcome of the fight far more than caliber. That's why Front Sight is a training institution and not a retail outlet.

NOT ONLY NO, BUT HELL NO

OVER my many years in firearms training, I have had a number of conversations which ended emphatically with "Not only no, but hell no!" Here are a few examples.

Back in May of 2001 we had yet another film crew at Front Sight. They had a list of demonstrations and interviews they wanted to capture on video. First was a subgun demo from me. Next on the schedule was a handgun demo from Naish. Knowing he had about 15 minutes until his performance, Naish went to an adjacent range to practice his presentations from the holster. I noticed his bladed stance was more like 45-50° instead of the 30° we profess. I turned to one of our Range Masters and said "Run over there and tell Naish his stance needs to be 30°." The little Scaredy-Cat told me "Not only no, but…"

Adam is our primary laborer and all-around helper in Alaska. He lives in Kenai, just down the road from our facility. He has an extremely modest lifestyle and lives in a cramped little house with his mom and all kinds of other people. Adam's sister is the family renegade because she had the gumption to move out of the house and get a job. Mind you, that job is working the pole at a strip dive named "Good Time Charlie's" in nearby Soldotna. This place is such a dump; complete with the faded plastic signs proclaiming "Cold Beer and Hot Girls." You know the deal. Adam had his 21st birthday last August and he invited the Front Sight staff out on the town (so we could pick up the tab, no doubt). I asked where he wanted to go. He said "Good Time Charlie's, we can watch sis dance!" I said "Not only no, but …"

Seeing "Good Time Charlie's" from the <u>outside</u> is plenty for me. Sorry, Adam…you and "sis" are on your own. August 2011.

In 2006 I got a call from a gentleman who described himself as an outdoor enthusiast. He had taken several firearms courses from us in the past and was now interested in ropes training so he could broaden his outdoor activities to include rappelling. He asked if he could attend the ropes course with his dog. I explained our policy of not having dogs on the property unless they were working dogs that were actually working. He said that he wanted his German Shepherd to be in the course with him. I told him that I didn't understand. He said "I want to get my dog into a harness and have him rappel off the tower, just like me. Can you guys do that?" I asked him in the friendliest voice possible "Are you saying you want us to teach your dog how to tie knots, set anchors, and rappel over the edge?" Boldly and without hesitation he said "Yes." Just as boldly and without hesitation, I said "Not only no, but…"

Back in the Bakersfield days, I had a handgun student who was visibly shaken on the range and I couldn't tell if he was mad, or sad, or what. I approached him to see if I could help. He asked if we could speak in private off to the side. I agreed and we went over the next range. Come to find out he was sad, and even depressed. With tears in his eyes, he told me how he and his wife had just separated and it looked like divorce was just around the corner. He really loved his wife and if he could figure out a way to convey that to her, maybe there was a chance they could stay together. He said to me "You are such a good speaker and you make your point so well, would you be willing to serve as a marriage counselor for me and my wife?" I politely replied "Not only no, but…"

Many moons ago, a fraternity buddy of mine signed me up for a bowling pin handgun competition known as a "pin match." I didn't even know what the hell that was. He explained "There will be five bowling pins standing on a table, seven yards away; haul out your .45 and knock 'em off. You do it twice. Whoever has the shortest time, wins." Wow, who was the creative genius behind this? Regardless, I went to the match. I was surprised just how serious these folks were. They even had special "pin loads" with sawtooth bullets. I guess the idea was that a serrated leading edge would somehow improve the performance of a 230-grain bullet traveling at 900 feet per second. Hmm. Anyway, it was my turn. The beeper sounded and I presented my 1911, fired five shots, and knocked down five pins. Next time, I did the same thing. Come to find out, I was the winner, by a margin of more than 10 seconds! I won the gold trophy and the $500 gift certificate, but not the favor of the local shooters. As I was leaving, five of these guys came out to the parking lot. They were visibly irritated and I thought briefly of the movie *Deliverance.* They asked me if I plan to ever come 'round these parts again. I happily said "Not only no, but…"

Jeff Cooper took a definite leap of faith in hiring me as a handgun instructor back in 1985. My first teaching assignment was in June that year and I was pretty excited. I drove onto the ranch the afternoon before class started and found the place completely quiet. I decided to check in at the "Gunsmithy" to socialize with Robbie Barrkman and his crew. Robbie was just preparing to test fire a 1911 he had been working on. We stepped out back to the little test-fire berm they had created behind the shop. Milling around behind the shop were maybe a dozen guinea hens which Mrs. Cooper had imported from South Africa. I had never before seen guinea hens and they looked to me like oversized gray chickens. Robbie told me that Janelle (Mrs. Cooper) likes to kill a couple of these birds for dinner on special occasions. He went on "This is definitely a special occasion; this is your maiden voyage as an instructor. You should shoot one for Mrs. Cooper." I was young, I was brand-new, and I really wanted to please the Cooper's. As such, I tried to find a safe angle to blast one of these birds and not hit anything else. About that time, Robbie said "Mrs. Cooper will be very impressed with you; guinea hens are hard to hit." That sounded strange. These damn birds were only 4-5 yards away, pretty big, and generally standing still. Robbie had seen me shoot, on many occasions. This was not a difficult shot. I ran the scene through my head…I knock on the Cooper's door with a limp guinea hen in my hand and proudly present it Janelle...only to find out I had just assassinated a member of her pet flock. Robbie asked "Well, are you going to shoot it?" I said "Not only no, but…"

I got a phone call from one of our students named Carl in the early-summer of 2005. Carl had recently divorced and was trying to orchestrate a fling with his high school girlfriend…of thirty years ago. Girlfriend spends summers in Anchor Point, Alaska which is maybe an hour and a half drive from our facility near Kenai. The only hurdle was those pesky kids of his. He asked, "Brad, would you be willing to put my kids in the 4-Day Children's course, let them sleep in a tent somewhere on-site, and give them some food on occasion, so I can go get laid?" I snapped "Not only no, but …"

I had just returned home from my very first handgun course under Jeff Cooper. I set all my stuff on the kitchen counter, including my 1911. Knowing that an unloaded gun makes a marginal club, I loaded up. My 19-year-old brother strolled into the kitchen and asked "How was it?" I replied how great it was and how much I had learned. He unexpectedly snatched my 1911 off the counter, quickly squatted down a little and opened his eyes wide for dramatic effect, put the muzzle against the side of his head, finger on the trigger, and growled "Did they teach you how to do this?" This was an era in our lives when my brother and I did not get along well. My mind raced to find just the perfect response which would cause him to press the trigger. However, my mother was standing right there, watching this scene, completely horrified. I calmly, peacefully, said "Not only no, but…"

During a recent Q&A session, I was asked about the acceptable delay between the end of a handgun course and the start of the subsequent CCW course. I responded that we are forced to comply with state regulations on this topic. Given our schedule of weekend and midweek courses, the maximum hiatus between handgun and CCW courses is six days. The various states are fine with six days, but they would not even consider something like 30 days. That's why our policy is that students must take the very next CCW following their handgun course. That very afternoon, a student approached our CCW guru, Scott Hoerner, with "Mr. Ackerman said in Q&A that I can get into CCW up to 30 days after my handgun course. Since I took the handgun course back in February, can I get into CCW tomorrow?" Scott immediately called me on the radio and he was pretty steamed, thinking I had flagrantly ignored the policy. "Did you tell this guy he could take the CCW course tomorrow?" I replied "Not only no, but…"

It was early-January in 1983 and I was driving back to college after Christmas break. My vehicle was completely full of guns, ammunition, archery gear, and clean clothes (thanks to Mom). My buddies and I were shooting in a handgun competition in less than a week and we needed to practice. We decided that unpacking the vehicle could wait and shooting could not. We headed to the wide open country south of Dallas and drove down a series of dirt roads until we were truly in the middle of nowhere. For targets, we stapled some brown paper bags onto the dead cottonwood trees and got busy shooting. This was perfect; we will have to remember this place. About that time, a gray, unmarked Crown Victoria skidded to a stop right behind my car. We were immediately looking down the muzzles of a 12-gauge shotgun and a .44 Magnum revolver, fingers all over the triggers. The .44 was shaking noticeably in the hands of the very young female officer and I later found out this was her very first day on the job. We were transported to Dallas County Jail for "unlawfully carrying a weapon." We were placed in the holding cell for processing and this was the only time in my life I had ever been in close proximity to such unseemly people. $200 in bail later, we were on our way. A couple days later, we got a call from an assistant DA who said something like "If you guys promise not to go shooting out in the woods again, we will drop the charges and you can come get your guns. Are you idiots going to pull this stunt again?" Collectively, we said "Not only no, but…"

In early-2012 I got an angry e-mail from a student who had taken lots of courses at Front Sight. In fact, he had taken six over the previous year alone. He was hopping mad that his most recent handgun course was completely different than his last, taken just a month earlier. "You guys added something new called the After Action Drills." I had to hear it straight from the horse's mouth so I called this guy personally. He asked me, "When did you guys add the After Action Drills?" I told him "in April…of 1996." He demanded "You didn't just add them last month?" I replied, "Not only no, but…"

I have a soft spot in my heart for those students who joined us for training in Alaska in the summer of 2004. We were still getting established up there but these students were willing to give us a try. One of the courses we offered was Alaska Outdoor Orientation which was designed to be a broad-brush overview of wildlife, rivers, glaciers, plants, geology, etc. I knew right away that the best "classroom" for this endeavor was floating down the Kenai River. I was armed with all my teaching aids like maps, photographs, binoculars, and, of course, fishing rods. My guests were a family of three from California who were fishermen, but not Alaska fishermen. Since this was not really designed as a fishing trip, I brought only two rods; each one equipped with an identical Pixie spoon. That's it, no other fishing gear. What's worse, I had fairly light line on these particular rods because we had already broken six rods that season and I didn't want to lose any more. We drifted into Morgan's Hole which is a sizeable eddy that holds lots of sockeyes. I dropped anchor in what seemed to be center stage and I made a quick cast. I showed everyone what a Kenai River sockeye looks like up close and then released the fish. Junior immediately asked if he could try. I gave him a rod and he flung the Pixie all the way to the shore and well into the trees. Now my arsenal consisted of a single Pixie. After a little heart-to-heart with Junior, he tossed the Pixie perfectly into the herd of fish. He yanked and instantly hooked one. He continued to yank, violently. Our last Pixie was a goner and I felt like a complete ass. What kind of fisherman brings a total of two lures? Junior asked "Do you have another Pixie?" Deflated, I had to admit, "Not only no, but…"

Way back when, a friend gave me a pair of Nelspot 007 paintball handguns. These things were quite primitive and the ammo was a joke. The individual paint balls were more egg-shaped than round and were filled with oil-based, pale-green paint. If you wanted even a semi-straight flight, you had to shake the paint balls thoroughly to mix the contents. I convinced Teresa, who at the time was my fiancé, to do a little "force-on-force" training. I would go hide in the bushes alongside the trail and she would come look for me. Classic Hunter vs. Hunted! When she strolled by I shot her square in the upper arm. Green paint was everywhere, but not enough to hide the serious welt. She asked me bluntly "Once we are married can I expect this crap to continue?" Sheepishly, I said "Not only no, but…"

I was working a handgun course under Jeff Cooper back in the late-'80's. I was low man on the totem pole and therefore had to stay after class to hang targets, paint steel, and empty trash. The students generally departed the range with vigor right at the end of the day, but on this particular day, one student lingered. He made a little idle conversation while I worked. When I was all done and ready to leave, he said very seriously and quietly, "Can I ask you a question? My wife and I are on the outs and we are likely going to get divorced. However, I have made a lot of money in recent years and I don't want that bitch to get any of it." He looked around to verify we were still alone and continued in a hushed tone "I know you have the skills...would you be willing to kill my wife for, say, $25,000?" I flatly told him "Not only no, but..."

Remember the Popeil Pocket Fisherman? It was the little, go-anywhere, plastic fishing rod advertised on TV back in the '70's and '80's. "Fits in the glove compartment and attaches to your belt...your personal fishing pal!" said the advertisements. Nobody who can even spell "fishing" would use such a thing beyond the koi pond. In 2009 we had a gentleman show up at Front Sight Alaska to take a Handgun Skill Builder course, after which he wanted to go fishing for kings. And he wanted to use his Popeil Pocket Fisherman! Alejandro desperately wanted to see the "personal fishing pal" literally explode, or possibly melt, in this guy's hands and begged me to say "Yes." However, I knew how tough it can be to even hook a 60-pound Kenai king, let alone land it. To go through all that effort with absolutely no chance of landing the fish seemed ridiculous. I told our fisherman that I highly recommended he use my king rods. That is what I said, but what I meant was "Not only no, but..."

We teach our students to handle their weapons the same way every time. Even simple administrative tasks should be conducted perfectly, crisply, as if your life depended on it. That way, you engrain nothing but perfect habits. For example, we encourage our students to present the weapon from the holster with gusto, every time, even if you are just going to set it on the night stand. One of our long-time students named Ron was en route to Front Sight and got pulled over by Nevada Highway Patrol for speeding. The officer asked Ron to step out of the car. As Ron stepped out, he mentioned that he was carrying a gun. The officer asked him to set in on the hood of the car. Ron snapped into action and presented from the holster briskly "as if to stop a gunfight," and damn near started one. Later that day, Ron told me his story. I told him there is a time and place for SLOW and deliberate gunhandling. Ron actually asked me "You mean you wouldn't have presented to the ready like I did?" I told him that I value my life too much. "Not only no, but…"

Since the first Glock handguns hit American soil in the mid-1980's, we have been hearing the same tired old jokes about "Combat Tupperware." At first, most folks were reluctant to give up their steel handgun and try one made of a high-tech polymer. That reluctance soon faded when the Glock proved to be such a superior weapon. But the Tupperware reference lived on. One of our new-hire Line Coaches named Mike, asked one of our seasoned Range Masters how best to clean his new Glock. The Range Master said "Like all Tupperware, it goes in the dishwasher. If it's really dirty, use the Pot Scrubber cycle." Everyone had a good laugh. The next morning Mike showed up and was clearly distressed. Indeed, he had run his Glock through the dishwasher and it emerged with a number of rusty parts. The frame was just fine because it's made of plastic and the slide was unharmed because of the Tenifer finish. But the sights, slide stop, and all the pins were bright orange with rust. Mike soon found the Range Master who had recommended the dishwasher. Mike told his tale of woe and concluded with "I even used Cascade, as you suggested. You were serious about all of this, weren't you?" The Range Master said "Not only no, but…"

Most exhibitors at conventions and trade shows just sit deep in their booths and wait for attendees to stroll in. Naish would never hear of such a thing. "The more you tell, the more you sell" he would say (with great regularity). Our method of working a show like SHOT or Safari Club was to get out of the booth and literally stop people in the aisles. "Have you heard of Front Sight?" we would ask people as we stepped directly in front of them. This approach was pretty aggressive, but it worked. We were able to slow people down and maybe even have a meaningful conversation. In 2000, we were working the Safari Club show in Reno. We were dressed in our usual gray and black uniforms, which were pretty militant for the soft, aristocratic crowd at that particular show. As part of our booth, we had an elevated platform where we were demonstrating various techniques with hunting rifles. True to form, we would step out in front of people and direct their attention to our rifleman up on the stage. Strolling down the aisle in our direction was a huddle of about 10 guys. Eight of them were clean cut, robust lads in their 30's and 40's, looking surly, and wearing black suits. The two distinguished older gentlemen right in the middle of the huddle were dressed more casually and looked friendlier than their counterparts. As the group approached, it became clear that the boys in black were Secret Service, and the two gents in the middle were former President George Bush and General Norman Schwarzkopf. One of our Range Masters asked me "Do you want me to step out in the aisle and stop these guys?" I said "Use your head! Not only no, but…"

TOW TRUCK AT THE READY

FRONT Sight Road is pretty nice. It is a smooth ribbon of asphalt which serves as our four-mile driveway. Dare I say, Front Sight Road is better than the roads adjacent to us which are maintained by the county. Sure, Front Sight Road is nice now, but let's turn back the hands of time and see what it was like in the early days.

I first saw our property in January of 1997. Naish and I were in Las Vegas to promote Front Sight at the SHOT Show, which is a big trade show for the shooting industry. After the convention wrapped up, we wanted to see the future home of Front Sight. Several of us squeezed into a rental car and headed west. We arrived in the general area with no problem, but getting to the actual property was a real challenge. 1997 was long before the existence of Front Sight Road and we had our choice of a few primitive, twisting, four-wheel-drive trails which snaked out into the desert. This was more like the Dakar Rally than a site visit. You have heard the old joke "What kind of car can go absolutely anywhere? A rental car!" God, I hoped that was true because we were certainly testing that theory. After numerous erroneous turns, and only one episode of "Get out and push," we arrived at the property. We strolled around, took photos, enjoyed a congratulatory hand shake, and then departed. Good thing the SHOT Show was over because our clothes were in no condition for public display.

We started running courses in Nevada two years later, in early-1999. The very first thing we needed to do was decide on which miserable route to take into the property. Old Spanish

Trail was the shortest but it crossed a couple of very steep ravines and had numerous splits and Y's, which made navigation difficult. Hidden Hills was a little bit flatter but it ran right through an old homestead which was abandoned, burned-out, and looked like a scene from a horror movie. Neither choice was very good. To make matters worse, both options were riddled with patches of very soft, 10-inch deep soil which resembled talcum powder. We cleverly called this soil "poof dirt." Eventually we settled on a combination of the two paths; the first couple of miles would be Hidden Hills, the last mile or so would be Old Spanish Trail.

We had numerous signs made up to keep people headed in the right direction. To mark the turnoff from the county road, we displayed a big, reflective, sandwich-board sign with the obligatory arrow. From that point on, we placed corrugated plastic signs at all the points of confusion. There, that oughta do it!

Not even close. On the very first morning of our very first course, we had a gentleman <u>walk</u> onto the property at about 10:00 a.m., literally covered from the waist down in "poof dirt." Seems he was driving his brand new, bright-yellow Corvette and he made it only as far as the poof dirt near the burned-out, single-wide trailers at Hidden Hills. By the time I met him, he was at wits end. After a brief chat, our would-be student and I got into my four-wheel-drive truck and we headed out to his Corvette. I backed my truck up to the nose of the Corvette in order to hook up a nylon tow strap. He politely asked me to hook the strap to the back end and tow him in the direction from which he came. As soon as his Corvette could move under its own power, he was going home! From that point on, I placed a staff member at the turnoff from the county road. He was equipped with a four-wheel-drive truck, a radio, a cell phone, and a tow strap. When someone needed rescuing, I simply called him on the radio. At 8:00, he would jump in the truck and drive back to the property, freeing any unlucky students from the La Brea Poof Dirt Pits along the way.

By mid-2000, we had all the engineering and bureaucratic work completed for Front Sight Road. I had never before been part of a road building project and I was shocked at the administrative hurdles:

- Consultants equipped with binoculars on the lookout for desert tortoises
- Dust control permits and the obligatory signs
- Staff trained in dust control practices (essentially how to properly run a garden hose)
- Permits to gently extract Yucca plants from the right-of-way and transplant them in the prescribed safe zone
- "Caution" tape, barricades, and warning signs

Man, this was tedious stuff but at least we were finally moving dirt. Cut, fill, compact. Cut, fill, compact. And so it went, for months, as Front Sight Road slowly took shape. By the end of 2000, the dirt work was complete. Front Sight Road was straight (except for one gentle bend), it was flat, and it was smooth. However, Front Sight Road was still just a dirt road and asphalt was another six months away. We did our level best to condition the road several times each day with the perfect amount of water. If done correctly, the water controlled the dust yet didn't create a muddy, slippery surface. That perfect balance was short-lived, and the desert sun soon returned the road to dry and dusty. Even so, our new road was glorious. Gone were the problems of getting lost in a horror movie, placing signs out in the desert, and keeping a tow truck at the ready.

My trusty "black" Lab named Argus. In May of 2000, I made the mistake of traveling down Front Sight Road with Argus in the back of my open truck!

"Straight, flat, and smooth" came with a distinct set of problems. It seems people were sick of traveling a paltry 10 miles per hour under the old conditions and now wanted to go 75 or 80. If all the conditions were just right, 75 miles per hour was manageable. However, if one tiny thing was amiss, someone was going into the ditch. Even a modest amount of traffic would change the hard-packed soil into dust and visibility would drop to zero. If just a touch of rain fell, the top ¼ inch of dirt would convert into axle grease. If a vehicle was traveling too fast and started to slide, especially on the curve, there was no recovery. We were averaging one serious accident per month. Most of the accidents followed the sequence of running late, driving too fast, start to slide, overcorrect, fly off into the ditch, and roll over a time or two.

As part of our EMT training, we had to work a couple of shifts riding along in the ambulance with the local paramedics. The idea here was to see some real-life action, not just books and PowerPoint presentations in the classroom. "Hell, I have already worked a dozen car crashes on Front Sight Road; may I please be excused from the ride-along?"

Pavement gave rise to yet another problem. And that problem was speed. Not just 85 or 90 miles per hour. No, that would be for women and little children. We had a former employee who leased a Nissan GT-R and turned it loose on Front Sight Road. He claimed 213 miles per hour was still quite comfortable inside that GT-R. I think this story contains some serious exaggeration, and might even be downright bullshit. He later smashed that car all to pieces, although thankfully without injury and not on Front Sight Road.

The guys with the "crotch rocket" motorcycles discovered Front Sight Road soon after it was paved. These guys were in hog heaven having just found a four-mile drag strip and they would gather in sizeable groups, particularly on Saturday mornings. I have no idea how fast these idiots would go, but it was fast; really, really fast. Just one little rabbit, or one little Front Sight student, would spell disaster. These guys were extremely cocky and completely out of control. They were not at all impressed with anything I had to say so I finally called Nye County Sheriff to run them off. I like to think I saved a life or two, but probably not. In all likelihood, they simply took their operation elsewhere.

Humans aren't the only ones who like Front Sight Road. So do the animals. Our limited supply of rainfall runs off the asphalt to the shoulder where it nourishes the plants. The vegetation attracts mice, squirrels, and rabbits from all around. The mice, squirrels, and rabbits attract snakes, foxes, and coyotes. This scene generally plays out best at night. And then there are the tarantulas. In mid-October every year, the tarantulas start their big migration. I have seen as may as 20 at one time over the length of Front Sight Road; Alfred Hitchcock would be proud. I have no idea where they go but they are always walking south and I have never seen them going back in the other direction. Maybe this is a one-way journey, ala the Pied Piper!

This tarantula was literally tiptoeing along the yellow brick road; right down the center stripe of Front Sight Road. October 2012.

So concludes the saga of Front Sight Road. It is now safe and sane; some would even say "boring." Perhaps that's true, and that's just the way the Operations Manager in me likes it.

CAN I CATCH A RIDE?

In April of 1996, we conducted our very first course in Bakersfield with a mere 10 students! That number has climbed straight up ever since. Back in the summer of 2007, Naish and I had a long conversation during which he described to me his marketing plans for the next 18 months. These plans, even if only 50% successful, would double our student numbers. It was clear; I needed to recruit more instructional staff.

The Instructor Development (ID) program was already in place and running beautifully. Also, there were lots of capable people out there in the world who might make good instructors for us. I just needed to bring the two together. If I could get lots of likely candidates in the seats for ID, we would be home free.

I got permission from Naish to cast a wide advertising net to gather as many ID candidates as possible. My "wide net" included:

- Full-page ads in the Las Vegas Review Journal
- Full-page ads in the L.A. Times
- Classified ads in the Pahrump Valley Times
- E-mail pitches to our entire list
- Flyers sent via snail mail to our entire list
- Booths at job fairs
- Postings at military bases in Las Vegas and Southern California
- Postings with Las Vegas Metro PD, Henderson PD, and Nye County Sheriff's Office
- Short presentations to students attending our regular courses

This advertising effort was an important test because it let me know which avenues to focus on in the future, and which ones to abandon. Each one of the above yielded different results, obviously. The one which drew the most attention was the L.A. Times, but these people were also the farthest away and the ads were quite expensive. Pitching directly to our students during courses yielded only small numbers but those who responded were <u>very good</u>. The job fairs and police departments were a complete bust; what a waste of time. E-mail was the most consistent producer because it was a very large venue of people already familiar with Front Sight. Without a doubt, the approach which provided the greatest number of stories, and migraine headaches, was the classified ad in the Pahrump Valley Times.

We ran the ad several different ways, but generally it read:

Firearms Instructors Wanted
Hiring part-time Defensive Handgun Instructors
Front Sight Firearms Training Institute, near Pahrump
Numerous part-time positions, possibly leading to full-time
Must have clean background and no visible tattoos
Military or Law Enforcement experience a plus, but not mandatory
Call Operations Manager Brad Ackman
(702) 555-5555

In preparation for the flood of calls, I built a big Excel spreadsheet so I could accurately record all of the data. My spreadsheet included a small "Notes" column at the end so I could jot down any relevant information which didn't handily fit into the other cells. After the first dozen calls, I realized the "Notes" column was way too small and was destined to become the most interesting.

As usual, I created a script which I used to guarantee every caller received the same delivery. I wanted a perfectly level playing field. Here is the outline form of my script:

Can I get your full name?

Are you familiar with Front Sight and what we do?
- We are a firearms training school
- 550 acres
- About 20 minutes outside of Pahrump
- Train thousands of students every year in defensive handgun, shotgun, rifle, etc.
- We have a large staff and we are always growing

We hire staff through a process called "Instructor Development"
- 4-day training course and audition
- This four-day effort involves no money:
  - We don't pay you
  - You don't pay us
- You get all the skills you need to be an instructor for us
- We get a look at your abilities
- If there is a match, we bring you on staff
- Right now hiring part-time handgun instructors
- Everyone starts as a handgunner, then cross-trains into shotgun, rifle, etc.
- We hire full-time staff from our pool of part-time instructors, so there is a possibility of full-time employment in the future

Starting pay is $X/hour. The next step up is $X/hour, and that usually comes within a month or two of being hired.

The next Instructor Development course in on (date).

Would you like to participate?

What you will need:
- Be at Front Sight at 7:30 on (date)
- 8-5, all four days

- Bring your defensive handgun, magazines, and holster
- Need 500 rounds of factory ammo
- Bring a lunch
- Map to the facility is at frontsight.com

You are all set! I have you on the roster for (date). I will call you again two days before the course to reconfirm.

Just to verify:
- We will run a background check on you. Is your background clean?
- We don't allow any visible tattoos. Is that a problem?

Additionally, I would like to offer you a free tune-up course:
- Get tuned-up before you take Instructor Development. This is certainly not mandatory, but might be helpful
- 2-Day or 4-Day Defensive Handgun
- Take your choice, or none at all
- FREE OF CHARGE
- Would you like to take that course? The next opportunity to take a free handgun course is on (date)

So, that was my script. It took me about 10-12 minutes on average to deliver it and handle all the questions. Over the coming months, I received 189 calls from our ad in the Pahrump Valley Times. As you can guess, I got pretty good at delivering that script! I had many friendly, intelligent conversations with the good folks of Pahrump. However, I also had some strange ones. Below are a few excerpts from my conversations with the odd-ball Pahrumpians.

Dan   "I don't need a tune-up course. I was a SEAL in the Army." (Yes, that's actually what he said.)

Richard   "Did you get the resume I sent to you at NRA.com?"

Dustin   "I am LDS with a DUI. And, I have a soccer scholarship."

Jonathan   "I spent a lifetime in the military; I hate guns, I wouldn't own a handgun. I'll be there."

Antonio   (Antonio, you sound pretty young. How old are you?) "14."

Tim   "Sorry, I live in Pahrump. You guys are too far away."

Michael   "Asking me if I can teach firearms is like asking Roger Clemens if he can pitch!"

Tony   "I would NOT have called had I known you were selling something. Damn it, I'm looking for a job!"

John   "Do I need to wear shoes?"

Willie   "I'll be ready 'cuz my old lady is gunna get me a G-Lock for Christmas." (Clearly Willie was confused by the Glock logo.)

Rick   "I am a 7th Day Adventist and my wife is LDS, so weekends are bad."

Harold   "I have a felony conviction, but it's because I was illegally carrying a gun. Certainly you guys can understand that, right?"

Jack   (I called Jack to confirm him for his free 4-Day Defensive Handgun course.) "Listen…I've had some legal troubles since we last spoke. A bogus domestic violence beef isn't enough to knock me out of the running, is it?"

Pablo (Pablo was talking, but it wasn't English, I have no idea what he said.)

James "I recently got a .45! I can buy 9mm ammo for it out there, right?"

Will "I don't own no gun, I don't have no internet. Teach…I can do."

Max "I used to have a felony conviction but that was a long time ago. I'm sure it's gone by now."

Chris "I don't have any experience, and I don't have a vehicle, but I read gun magazines EVERY month."

David "Do you guys offer medical benefits? I have pretty severe arthritis and cataracts I'd like to get fixed."

Aaron "I am ready right now. I mean RIGHT NOW!"

Dennis "Should I bring a sleeping bag and a change of clothes?"

Angelo "I need to ask my wife. She's not big on killing people."

Juan "Tell me again how much you are going to pay me for this interview. Can I get that in cash?"

Carol "No thanks, I don't need a tune-up course. I have my CCW."

John (John had called and left me a message. I returned his call and a lady answered. I explained who I was and that I was calling about possible employment for John.) John hollered from the background, "Tell him I'll call him back at halftime."

Allen   "My house arrest is up in a month. This should work out just right."

Jessica   "Do you guys provide daycare? That's okay; they will be fine in the car."

Dex   "I have tats all over my neck. But I can cover 'em with the old lady's makeup."

Tim   "I'm pretty good with guns, even thought I haven't shot one in a good-long while. In fact, the only time I ever shot a gun was when Grandma let me shoot her .22 down at the ranch."

Mike   "Okay, I'll be there on Friday the 22nd. Oh, one last thing. Can I catch a ride with you that morning?"

Damien   "Can I bring my granddad along as my advisor?"

Darrel   "Maybe I should start slow and take a children's course."

Woman calling on behalf of someone else   She yelled across the room, "Honey, honey I got him on the phone! Get your lazy ass off the couch!"

Chaz   "Hell, I've shot hundreds of people stone dead. I don't need tunin' up."

Marvin   (Marvin was speaking English, but it was so mushy that I couldn't understand a single word. I honestly think he had no teeth.)

Tyrone   "Does the bus run out to Front Sight?"

Dick   "Can we do this interview at my house instead?"

Sal   "It would be an honor to work with the Michigan Militia."

By January of 2008, I couldn't take it anymore. Honestly, I felt my IQ slip every time I answered the phone. After about four months, I passed the project over to one of our Range Masters named Jim, along with the script. Together we answered about 25 calls side-by-side, just to be sure he was squared-away. In about a week, Jim called me and said "You will never guess the crazy shit I hear from these Pahrump people!" God, I was happy they were calling Jim and not me.

Just to be fair, we did hire some high-quality people through our ad in the Pahrump Valley Times. In fact, several of them aspired to Range Master and even Senior Range Master. See, they weren't all knuckle-dragging, mouth-breathing, illiterate, convicted felons without transportation.

NAZI BOY SCOUTS

We wear a very specific, highly regimented uniform at Front Sight. The uniform is composed of a gray military-style shirt with the obligatory creases and epaulets, black BDU-style pants which are bloused at the top of the boots, black uniform/duty boots, and a black baseball cap with the Front Sight logo. Add to that embroidered name tapes above the pockets and all sorts of hardware around the waistline.

Brad Ackman wearing the Front Sight uniform and shooting a demonstration during a 4-Day Defensive Handgun course in April 2000.

When worn correctly, the Front Sight uniform looks crisp, distinguished, and serious. Sounds good, but lots of folks still complain about it. The usual complaints are:

- Too hot, especially the black hats in the summer
- Too dark, especially the black pants
- Shows too much dust and dirt
- Too formal
- Too intimidating
- Impersonal with the instructor's <u>last</u> name above the pocket
- Unapproachable; should have the instructor's <u>first</u> name as well
- Too militant, especially the epaulets on the shoulders, creases in the shirts, and bloused pants
- Too old-school; should be more modern, like a golf pro
- Screen printing on the back of the shirt wears off
- The gray shirts fade in the sun to a light purple
- Etc., etc., etc. Bitch, bitch, bitch.

In addition to the above list, three more complaints come to mind. The very first complaint about the Front Sight uniform came from Chuck Taylor. Chuck was with Front Sight at the very beginning, but his time with us was short-lived and he has long since departed. He felt the uniform was too revealing of one's curves. You must realize that Chuck used to be a strapping young lad with broad shoulders and a thin waist. Age has a way of reversing things. The extra pounds didn't reduce Chuck's skill at all, but he was certainly self-conscious about his appearance. So much so, he demanded to wear a different uniform than the rest of us. (So much for uniformity.) From the belt down, Chuck's garb was the same as the rest of us. Above the waist, Chuck was completely different. Instead of a button-up uniform shirt, properly tailored and tucked in, he opted for T-shirt worn under a BDU-style jacket which he wore unbuttoned, untucked, and with the sleeves rolled up to mid-forearm. Additionally, he had the dry cleaners apply enough starch to his jackets that they bordered on straight jackets. The result was a rigid gray tube which connected his head to his legs, and did NOT show any curves. Chuck also bucked the long-standing etiquette of placing the name of the organization, in this case "Front Sight," above the left pocket. The idea here is the name of the organization, team, or unit is placed over your heart, because it is of greater importance than the individual. The name of the individual is placed above the right pocket. Not for Chuck. The coveted spot over his heart always read "Taylor."

Naish likes the appearance of our uniforms but he is not fond of purchasing them. The amount of money we have spent on uniforms since 1996 is shocking. Each Instructor receives four pants, four short-sleeve shirts, four long-sleeve shirts, two hats, and a jacket. This package costs in the neighborhood of $450, complete with screen printing and embroidery. We have issued almost 500 sets of uniforms over the years. That's pretty easy math, and it totals $225,000. Most folks don't understand the ramifications of "Get rid of those uniforms and start over!"

The most enthusiastic slam of the Front Sight uniform came from a lady who took a 4-Day Defensive Handgun course with us in 2004. She loved the training but abhorred the uniform, saying, "You guys look like Nazi Boy Scouts!" Wow, I don't even know what a "Nazi Boy Scout" is, but it doesn't sound good. Moreover, I am not sure what to do about that.

I suppose all the above uniform complaints fall squarely into the category of "you can't please everyone." True, if we were to select a uniform from scratch today it might be different than what we selected in 1996. However, we would definitely still wear a uniform, and it would still be crisp and professional. It is with significant pride that I look at a range full of people and see the black and gray uniforms standing boldly above a sea of T-shirts and faded jeans.

Understand, this entire discussion about uniforms is pretty irrelevant in the big picture. People come to Front Sight for training, and skill, and confidence. They don't come to Front Sight because of what the staff looks like. As long as we continue to positively impact our students, I can live with being called a "Nazi Boy Scout."

THIS IS BEAR COUNTRY

WARNING: This chapter contains some... well... technical gun stuff. If you have an interest in such things, please continue. If not, STOP! Turn to the next chapter and don't look back.

Alaska is certainly "bear country." However, that doesn't mean the bears are thick and problematic. In fact, many tourists arrive in Alaska each summer hoping to see a bear but go home with pictures of moose and massive cabbages instead. There are indeed some hot-spots where brown/grizzly bears concentrate at certain times of the year, generally to fill up on sockeye salmon. Such places include Brooks Falls, McNeil River, and Kodiak Island. However, the Kenai Peninsula, which is home to Front Sight Alaska, is not overrun with bears. Yet, it only takes one! And that's enough to keep the discussions, urban legends, and great debates alive.

The classic debate surrounding bears in Alaska is "what is the ideal gun to stop a charging grizzly?" Many options have been proposed and all have proven successful at one time or another. If you ask the gun store clerk, he will likely direct you to the gun which he currently has too many of. If you ask the weathered ol' homesteader, he will likely suggest a rusty .30-06 because that's what he owns and besides, he once shot a bear stone-dead with it. If you consult the shooting and outdoor magazines, you will <u>never</u> get an answer because the job of the magazine editor is not to settle debates, but rather to perpetuate them and sell magazines.

One of the most thorough and quantitative efforts I have seen to determine the correct weapon for bear defense was from the United States Geological Survey (USGS). Some number of years ago, the USGS studied the subject after they lost a couple of staff members to bears in Alaska. They subsequently published a very impressive report which considered all sorts of gun-related factors including ease of use, reliability under field conditions, availability of ammunition out in the bush, and most importantly, the likelihood of stopping a charging bear. The USGS concluded that a 12-gauge shotgun loaded with slugs was the most appropriate choice. However, the USGS went two steps further. They acknowledged the importance of proper training and the need for a designated shooter.

Well then, does that conclude the great debate? Is the ubiquitous 12-gauge pump shotgun loaded with slugs the ultimate bear stopper? While that combination certainly works, it is not the best answer for everyone. By far the most important element in the equation is the operator. I would much rather be in the field with a seasoned, level-headed professional armed with a crappy gun, than with a skittish neophyte armed with a cannon. As such, a proper discussion about "bear stoppers" must also include the operator. I propose for your consideration, my top three choices of bear stoppers.

Third Place: .375 H&H Bolt Action Rifle

A bolt action rifle chambered in .375 H&H Magnum is a good bear stopper. It has widespread popularity in Alaska for bears but also in Africa as defense against troublesome lions, buffalo, and the like. It works well.

Pros:

A big bolt rifle in the hands of a capable shooter is a serious weapon. Probably the best all-around rifle caliber for bear defense is .375 H&H because it is widely available, hits extremely hard, and has excellent penetration. However, any caliber in the .375 to .416 range will suffice. Also, a .375 bolt rifle can pull double duty as both a hunting rifle and a defensive weapon. By far the most common caliber among deer hunters on

Kodiak Island is .375 H&H. Certainly a .375 is gross overkill for a Sitka Blacktail deer, but a .243 doesn't cut it against a charging brown bear. Since nobody wants to carry two guns, go for the big one. 'Tis better to have it and not need it…

Cons:

A .375 H&H bolt rifle recoils pretty hard, especially with a lightweight synthetic stock. The Remington XCR is a great field rifle, in part because it has a thin contour barrel and a lightweight synthetic stock. It is also one of the hardest recoiling rifles I have ever fired. There is very little chance that ANYONE is going to practice much with that contraption. And that's a real problem because training is critical. If you are scared of the gun, you won't train with it, and you will find yourself afield with limited skill and confidence.

Another drawback to the bolt rifle is the fact that it's a bolt rifle. In other words, you must run the bolt. This mechanical complexity seems like a small issue when you are warm, dry, and calm. However, running the bolt flawlessly under stress can be a challenge, unless your muscle memory runs deep. Again, this is merely a training issue…but it's a big issue.

Ammunition capacity is also on the "cons" list. Most magnum bolt rifles hold only three rounds; one in the chamber and two in the magazine. You can probably…maybe…get the job done with three rounds.

Setting Up Your Bear-Stopping Rifle

Here are a few considerations when setting up a bolt rifle for defense against bears.

- ACTION. It's nice to have a controlled feed action, such as a Winchester Model 70. "Controlled feed" means the round coming out of the magazine is held securely by a big, claw-like extractor. With this system, double feeds caused by short-stroking are less likely and extraction is generally flawless. Controlled feed is not mandatory, however. If you already own a Remington 700, there is no need to go shopping. I consider stainless steel to be mandatory. These days, why would anyone bother with blued steel for a field gun?

107

- CALIBER. The caliber should be hard hitting and readily available in far-flung places like Naknek or Cold Bay. .375 H&H fills the bill nicely. Other calibers such as .375 Remington Ultra Mag., .378 Weatherby, .416 Remington, and .416 Rigby are even more potent than .375 H&H but the ammo can be tough to find out in the bush.
- AMMUNITION. As you well know, not all ammo is created equal and it must be properly matched to the task. I really like Federal Premium because the quality is consistently sky-high, which helps boost confidence. The nickel plated case is also a plus. Federal offers a couple of different bullets and I prefer the 300-grain Barnes Triple Shock because it penetrates very well, even after hitting heavy bone. For what it's worth, this particular load is also very accurate. I have shot numerous groups under one inch from all three of my .375's. Accuracy is irrelevant at 10 yards against a charging grizzly, but it is nice on a 300-yard deer or caribou shot taken in bear country.
- BARREL LENGTH. 24-inch barrels are the industry standard and are just fine. A 22-inch barrel might be a touch better for a defensive rifle because it is compact and handy. Longer barrels, say 26 inches or so, yield slightly higher muzzle velocity but are a bit heavier and more cumbersome.
- SIGHTS. Open sights are the way to go. Remember, we are talking about a defensive rifle, not necessarily a hunting rifle. The exact style of iron sights is not as big an issue as some profess. If you like traditional rifle sights, great. If you prefer a ghost ring, that too is fine. Make sure they are easily visible in low light. They also need to be sufficiently robust to stay on the rifle during hard field use. Set your iron sights for dead-on at 10 yards, not 100!
- STOCK CONFIGURATION. Synthetic is preferable to wood, obviously. Keep the stock short enough to work well with rain jackets, chest waders, and backpack straps. When in doubt, go shorter. Also, consider the smallest

person who will be using the weapon. The big dude can easily use the shorter stock. The petite lady cannot easily use the longer stock.

- ILLUMINATION. We all carry flashlights with our handguns but almost nobody mounts a flashlight to their bolt rifle. A flashlight attached to the stock certainly looks odd, I grant you. But Rule 4 mandates "Be sure of your target." To do that, you have to see the target! I simply attach a small rail to the support side of the stock and use the light from my Glock. (All tactical handgun lights come with the mounting system built in.) Angle the light properly and it will illuminate the target <u>and</u> the front sight. I like the Streamlight TLR-1 because it is compact, has a bright LED bulb, is made of aluminum instead of plastic, and is easy on batteries.

A standard Weaver-style scope mount which fits the contour of the stock works perfectly as a flashlight base. For this application, I rounded the edges of the mount ("dehorning"), then plated it with hard chrome, and attached it with stainless steel screws.

Attach the flashlight to the mount and you are ready to use the open sights in low-light conditions. Make certain you can properly see the open sights over the scope base.

- CHEEK PAD. A good cheek pad from Black Hawk or Eagle has external ammunition loops which means you can carry spare ammo <u>on the weapon</u>. Also, a good cheek pad allows easier sight alignment. The zippered pouch gives you a place to store spare flashlight batteries and the like. With a cheek pad, the entire package becomes a "grab-and-go" proposition. The old leather "butt cuffs" of yesteryear, such as those made by Milt Sparks and Bruce Nelson, are a no-go because the leather loops soon lose their ability to securely hold ammo.
- SLING. If you are simply going to use the rifle as a camp gun, you don't need a sling. That seems pretty unlikely, however. More likely, you will be carrying the rifle with you for some portion of the day. I like a simple carry strap made of 1¼" nylon webbing (not cotton) and plastic hardware (not metal).

- AMMUNITION CAPACITY. You can increase the ammo capacity by one round if you switch out the "bottom metal" (the assembly which constitutes the magazine box, floor plate, and trigger guard). The ammo capacity becomes four rounds instead of three. For your Remington, this can be done with the detachable magazine system made by H-S Precision. For your Winchester, this can be done with a "drop belly" assembly made by Sunny Hill and then a new stock by McMillan. I place this item last on the list because it offers only a modest improvement and comes at a high price.

Setting Up Your Dual-Purpose Rifle

As I mentioned above, the real plus of a bolt rifle is that it functions well as both a hunter and a fighter. Hunting and self defense are similar in that you need to get good hits in a timely manner. However, the circumstances between the two situations are quite different. The hunting shot is taken at a time dictated by the hunter and usually at a significant distance. The hunting shot favors a scope. The defensive shot is always taken at a time dictated by the animal and always at close range. The defensive shot favors open sights. Clearly, a dual-purpose rifle needs both a scope and open sights.

Let's assume you are out hunting. You will have the scope on the rifle and the flashlight in your backpack. When you are done hunting for the day, you will be back in camp sitting around the fire. Simply take the scope off the rifle and put the flashlight on. Now you are ready for the proverbial bump in the night. It's very easy to add or remove the scope and flashlight if both are equipped with a high-quality quick-detach (QD) system. Ah, but what if you are out hunting and are surprised by a bear? There is obviously no time to remove the scope. As long as you purchased the correct scope, you will be fine.

Let me cut to the chase and describe some of my favorite equipment. As for QD scope mounts, there are two brands which eclipse all the rest; Talley and Seekins. The Talley system is available in stainless steel and uses a handy thumb lever for easy on and off. The Seekins system is very robust, fabricated of aluminum, and requires an Allen wrench to remove. With either of these setups, you can install and remove your scope a hundred times and it will always stay sighted in. Make certain you can still see the iron sights over the scope bases once the scope is removed. Also, using 8-40 screws to attach the bases is a good idea because they are a bit more robust that the 6-48 version. And remember, this rifle is a sledgehammer, not a family heirloom.

Now for the scope. I suggest the following features.

- VARIABLE POWER. The range of 1-5 or 2-8 is about right. The low-end magnification is the most important; the smaller the better. Carry the rifle with the scope on the lowest setting. That way, if you face a surprise attack, using the scope is fast and easy. If you see a trophy deer a couple hundred yards out, run the magnification up to a higher setting. After the shot, run the magnification back down! The guys who routinely hunt Kodiak and Afognak are fond of saying the rifle shot is a "dinner bell" heard far and wide by the bears. The bears know that a fresh meal awaits and numerous encounters happen right after the shot is made. <u>Run your scope back down to the lowest magnification ASAP.</u>
- 30mm TUBE. The fatter tube allows for greater light transmission. Bears are like bad guys; they generally come out in low light.
- ILLUMINATED RETICLE. Black cross hairs against black hair are tough to see, and thus slow to use. Bright, flaming-red cross hairs against black hair are very fast.
- CLEAR LENS CAPS. Protect your lenses with clear, see-through caps. Don't try to face a charging bear with black lens caps that are snapped shut.

I like Leupold and they make a couple of scopes in the Mark 4 MR/T series with the above features. Leupold is obviously not the only game in town, but they are probably the best when considering the above criteria.

My preferred scope for a dual-purpose bear rifle (hunting and self-defense) is the Leupold Mark 4 MR/T with 2.5-8 magnification and illuminated TMR reticle. This particular rifle is equipped with the Seekins scope mount system. The Seekins components are beautifully machined and the one-piece base has a recoil lug at the forward edge of the ejection port; ideal for heavy-recoiling rifles.

With see-through scope caps, you are prepared to shoot even if the caps are closed. If you have the luxury of time, simply flip up the scope caps for a better view and turn on the illuminated reticle.

Second Place: 12-Gauge Shotgun

The 12-gauge shotgun has stopped a lot of charging bears. It has stood the test of time and is the default "bear medicine" in Alaska.

Pros:
There are lots of reasons why a 12-gauge shotgun loaded with proper slugs is a good choice in bear country. Chief among them…it works! A 12-gauge slug has only about half the energy of a .375 H&H, but it still works well at stopping bears, moose, and similar problems. What's more, the shotgun holds about twice the ammo of a .375 bolt rifle. Which would you rather have, three rounds or six? Shotguns are affordable, readily available, and fairly easy to run. There is also a wide array of 12-gauge ammunition available in addition to slugs. For example,

114

put a few rounds of birdshot in your pack for ptarmigan or ducks. And carry a few 12-gauge signal flares for emergency use, just in case.

Cons:

The "cons" list for a 12-gauge shotgun is pretty short. Training with a shotgun is fairly easy, certainly easier than a bolt action rifle. However, training is still needed. If you are using a pump-action shotgun, running the action had better be second nature. If you short stroke the action during a bear charge, you are truly screwed. A semi-auto takes care of all that.

Ammo Selection:

One nice thing about 12-gauge shotguns is the huge variety of ammunition. There are the obvious loads like birdshot, buckshot, and slugs. But there are other nifty loads like duplex shot loads, "cracker rounds," screamer/whistler rounds, rubber bullets, bean bags, and flares. Some shooters are dazzled by the large array of ammo choices and end up getting too clever in their selection. I have heard numerous times of people loading their bear defense shotgun with a staggered offering of birdshot, buckshot, and slugs. The idea here is that if a menacing bear gets too close, a load of birdshot may prompt him to retreat because he was scared by the noise, or irritated by the "sting" on his skin, or even blinded by the shot. If the bear is not impressed by the birdshot, the next load in the magazine is buckshot, usually 00 Buck. The idea here is that you are now shooting heavier projectiles which should penetrate better and you still get the benefit of a pattern. Should the 00 Buck fail to stop the now-irritated-and-charging bear, the rest of the magazine contains slugs. This "last ditch" load will likely penetrate well and marksmanship is generally not a problem because the bear is now mere inches from the muzzle! "Skip loading" is a silly approach to bear defense and I'm sure it was dreamed up over a bottle of Jack Daniels while sitting around some campfire. Sheer stupidity. A similarly poor idea is starting with a flare or "cracker round" as a scare tactic and then graduating to more serious loads.

The answer to all this is "keep it simple." Slugs are definitely the proper round for bear defense. However, not all slugs are the same. The standard, domestic, Foster-style, soft lead slugs are cheap to practice with but are not up to the task of stopping a charging brown bear. Standard slugs run the risk of breaking apart if they hit bone, thus reducing penetration. The Brenneke design is the one you want. This slug is made of a hard alloy and penetrates extremely well. A cop friend of mine in east Texas tells a story of having to shoot a Brahma bull after it escaped from the rodeo and was wandering the streets goring all of the parked cars. He arrived on the scene carrying a shotgun loaded with Brenneke slugs. He fired one shot into the chest of the big bull from about 10 yards away. The round went through-and-through and poked a big hole in a Corvette parked on the other side. The owner of the Corvette was none the wiser because the 12-gauge hole blended nicely with all the other holes made by the bull. The bull took one step and slumped to the ground.

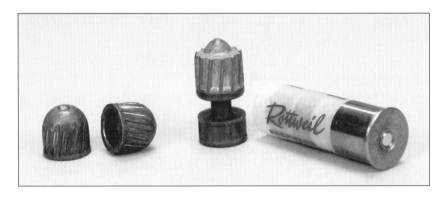

Standard shotgun slugs (left) are just right for training, but just wrong for bear defense. Brenneke slugs (center and right) are a much better choice because they are very hard and penetrate well.

Comparison to .375 H&H

So, why does a 12-gauge shotgun rate higher than a .375 H&H bolt rifle for bear defense? While both will stop a charging bear with proper ammunition and proper shot placement, the 12 gauge holds more ammo, has softer recoil, is easier to run and therefore promotes confidence, is cheaper to purchase, and ammunition is available just about everywhere.

Setting Up a Shotgun for Bear Country

Some things to consider when setting up a defensive 12-gauge shotgun:

- ACTION. Your two choices are pump or semi-auto. I prefer semi-autos and I like the old Benelli M-1 Super 90 (or the current M-2). Pumps are cheaper and equally reliable...if you train with them. Remington 870 and Mossberg 590A1 are the frontrunners. Unfortunately, none of these shotguns are available in stainless steel.
- GAUGE. 12 gauge is just right. 10 gauge hits harder but proper ammo is tough to find and recoil is a little much. 20 gauge is not potent enough.
- BARREL LENGTH. Barrels in the 18-20 inch range are just right because they are compact and easy to use. Choke tubes in the barrel are just fine as long as they are tight. Use the "Improved Cylinder" choke tube.
- AMMUNITION. 2¾ inch is probably better than 3 or 3½ inch because recoil is more manageable and ammunition capacity is higher. Brenneke USA and Rottweil both make great ammo loaded with Brenneke slugs. I prefer the Rottweil and twice I have shot a clover leaf group at 50 yards from my Benelli with open sights.
- SIGHTS. Beads are bad. Repeat after me...beads are bad! There are so many good shotgun sights to choose from including ghost rings, large pistol-style sights, and tritium, don't settle for a bead.
- STOCK CONFIGURATION. Synthetic and short, just like the rifle discussion. Folding stocks, pistol grips, and pistol forends are problematic.
- ILLUMINATION. Just like the rifle discussion...
- CHEEK PAD. Just like the rifle discussion...
- SLING. Just like the rifle discussion...

- AMMUNITION CAPACITY. You should bump up the ammo capacity as much as reasonably possible. The Benelli is already equipped with a longer magazine tube. If you select a pump gun, install a Scattergun Technologies magazine tube. More ammo is better. Some people argue about weight and balance, but ammo capacity is senior to either of those, by a wide margin.

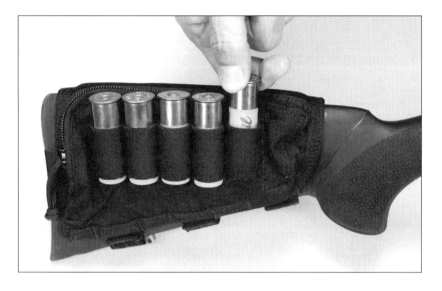

A high-quality cheek pad, like this one from Black Hawk, serves more functions that just carrying ammo.

This Remington 870 is properly set up for bear defense. It has a 20-inch barrel, Scattergun Technologies extended magazine tube, Trijicon night sights, Black Hawk cheek pad, rounded recoil pad for snag-free mounting, and a weatherproof, hard chrome finish. On the support side of the gun (not visible in this photo) is a Streamlight TLR-1 flashlight mounted on the forend.

Winner: OC and a Glock 23

Such heresy! How could a "gun guy" possibly prefer pepper spray? And what's with a Glock 23? Well, here's the background...

I was in graduate school in Missoula, Montana in 1988. A Missoula-based company called Counter Assault, was just unveiling the very first pepper spray ever to hit the market. Counter Assault had developed their product in close coordination with the University of Montana and the National Park Service. One day I saw a poster on campus advertising a lecture being given by the guys from Counter Assault. The poster briefly discussed the product which was a spray made from hot pepper extract (oleoresin capsicum or "OC"). I was long familiar with mace, but I had never heard of OC. According to the poster, OC had shown great promise as a bear deterrent. "Wishful thinking," I thought. "Let me get this straight. I am hiking in the woods. I look up and see an angry 800-pound grizzly charging directly at me like a freight train. I spray him with a Tabasco-like solution and the bear not only stops dead in his tracks, but he actually runs away?" Yep, that's pretty much it. I attended the lecture completely prepared to be the pro-gun heckler, if the opportunity arose.

The lecture started with the obligatory background information and then quickly focused on the field trials of the pepper spray. Counter Assault had just concluded a six-year program to create a non-lethal bear deterrent. They cited numerous cases (complete with video documentation) where they had sprayed dozens of problem bears with OC. The results were impressive, dare I say convincing. However, Counter Assault OC was not widely available at the time. A year later, in the spring of 1989, the Exxon Valdez oil tanker ran aground in Alaska's Prince William Sound and workers from all over the world converged to start the clean up. Counter Assault sold thousands of cans of their bear deterrent to Exxon. That one event literally put OC on the map.

The field work portion of my Master's thesis was in Glacier National Park, which is celebrated bear country. I would be in the backcountry of Glacier for weeks at a time and I needed some sort of weapon. Even with the convincing field trials, and the dozens of success stories coming out of Prince William Sound, I was still a "gun guy." Since the National Park Service staunchly prohibited carrying weapons inside park boundaries, I was relegated to a handgun which I could conceal. Smith & Wesson had just recently introduced a three-inch, stainless .44 Magnum which I was pretty sure I could conceal when I was near civilization. That revolver was my closest friend for weeks at a time. I encountered numerous bears in Glacier during those two summers but each and every encounter ended peacefully.

This begs the question of carrying a handgun for bear protection. No reasonable handgun caliber is sufficient for use as bear defense. Only the .500 S&W with a long barrel produces enough energy to even approach that of a shotgun slug (and both are well short of a .375). Toting around a heavy, long-barreled revolver, only to deliver less ballistic performance, is a step in the wrong direction. I carried a handgun because it was all I could manage, not because it was the best choice.

It wasn't until I moved to Alaska in 1990 that I routinely carried pepper spray. I worked for a sizable environmental engineering firm and our client list included the State of Alaska, Army Corps of Engineers, Federal Aviation Administration, and the National Park Service. I spent most of my time in remote Alaska studying various contaminated sites and carrying OC. Over the years since 1990, I have had occasion to spray all sorts of animals including bears, moose, dogs, and people. It has always worked. More important than my own experiences are the hundreds of field accounts supporting the claim that OC is an extremely effective, non-lethal, bear deterrent.

I don't know of a single occurrence where a bear was sprayed in the face with OC and continued to fight. I know of several occurrences where the bear was sprayed in the chest or neck with OC and there was no effect. Some folks point to these as OC failures. Understand that you must hit the eyes and nose to stop the bear (or moose, or dog, etc.) When a bear is charging you, the face is always front and center. Therefore, the face is an easy target, especially given the massive, thick fog of OC that comes out of the can. I acknowledge that if a bear takes you from behind, unaware, it will be nearly impossible to deploy your OC. The same goes for a firearm. We certainly cannot blame the OC for that.

Some people disparage OC because you might accidentally spray yourself, or get some on you if the wind is blowing. True, if you are careless, you might spray yourself and it will burn for a while. If you are careless with a .375, you might also shoot yourself. How would that be?

Speaking of poor "can handling," I was on an oil-spill site in western Alaska with a sizeable field crew. We rented several 15-passenger Ford vans from the local Native corporation to haul our staff and all our overpriced equipment (purchased with your tax dollars). Late in the day, we had a bear walk right through our soil sampling grid so we backed up and had OC at the ready. After the bear departed peacefully, one of the young ladies in our group neglected to replace the little safety clip on her OC. At the end of the day, nine people climbed into the van with this lady. As she sat down, she discharged her entire can of OC into the van. I thought all of this was hilarious since I was watching from a different van, and breathing fresh air! That evening at dinner we all had a good laugh. This lady had made a huge mistake with her OC and the worst that came of it were some bloodshot eyes. I'll take those odds any day.

OC works. In addition, OC is readily available just about everywhere including grocery stores, hardware stores, and tackle shops, far and wide. I hate to even say it, but OC is also politically correct. Walk into a restaurant in Kenai with a can of OC on your belt and people won't even notice. And if they do notice, the general image of people carrying OC is that of "outdoor enthusiast," or "fisherman just off the water." Walk into that same restaurant with a 12-gauge shotgun slung over your shoulder and see what reaction you get. In all likelihood, you will get stopped at the door, even in gun-friendly Kenai. OC is also very easy and intuitive to use by the non-warriors in your family. You can hand a can of OC to your mother or daughter and feel confident about it. That's not the case with a .375 bolt rifle. OC is also inexpensive. You can cheaply equip every member of your family, and the boat, and the truck, etc. You can literally hand it out like Halloween candy! And having multiple people all sporting cans of OC is a real comfort. OC is small, light, and easy to carry. It is no more burdensome than carrying a can of Red Bull (which you should also have). Therefore, OC is easy to keep with you, typically on your belt, as you go about your day. Rifles and shotguns are set down at every opportunity because they are big and heavy. Notice a group of hikers or fishermen setting out in the morning carrying a rifle or shotgun for bear defense. The designated gun bearer is perky, alert, and the gun is at the ready. An hour later, that same gun is slung over a shoulder. By lunch, that gun is poked deep into the backpack alongside the raingear. I wonder; what is the time necessary to stop, take off the backpack, pull out the shotgun, aim, and fire?

OC works beautifully on animals. OC works pretty well on humans, except for the dopers and the psych patients. That's where the Glock 23 comes in. The Glock 23 is chambered in .40 S&W and has an excellent record of stopping bad guys. Hateful animals get the OC; hateful people get the Glock 23. My normal setup while fishing in Alaska is a can of OC on my belt and a Glock 23 concealed in the front pouch of my waders. This arrangement is comfortable to carry all day and raises no eyebrows.

So, there you have my suggestion. While out doing your thing in bear country, carry a can of OC and a Glock 23. (That even rhymes a little.) I know that my opinions are in no way definitive and probably produce more arguments than answers. Well, let the debate begin. The proper forum for such a conversation is obviously while sitting around the campfire…near a salmon stream in bear country…with a can of OC on my belt.

Hmm...choices, choices. .375 H&H (left), 12-gauge Brenneke slugs (center), the combination of .40 S&W and OC (right), and a perplexed, overly-analytical "thinker" in the background.

HOME BREW

FACTORY ammunition certainly isn't perfect. In fact, I have amassed quite a collection of misfit rounds which came right out of factory boxes produced by Winchester, Remington, Federal, and the like. I have seen bullets installed upside down, primers installed upside down, primers missing altogether, cases cracked, cases crumpled down one side like an accordion, and errant rounds of .40 in a box of .45. Yep, even the big boys screw it up on occasion.

Here are some of the defective handgun rounds I have collected over the years. Deformed bullets, smashed cases, inverted primers, and inverted bullets are not the norm from the factory...but they do exist.

But even with these very-rare flaws, factory ammunition is FAR superior to most home-brew reloads. The reason is quality control. The big ammunition manufacturers have multiple layers of quality control while the guy out in the garage has one, or perhaps, none. The one exception to all of this is custom, hand-loaded, centerfire rifle ammunition which is being paired to a specific rifle. In this scenario, the person doing the work is inspecting each primer, measuring each piece of brass, checking each bullet, and weighing each powder charge. After the round is built, it is measured again to verify the overall length is exact. That level of care results in a quality product.

That level of care however, is not the norm in reloading. The reason most people reload is to save money. Therefore, they purchase inexpensive components such as once-fired brass, off-brand bullets, and whatever powder is on sale. Then they sit down at their unsophisticated reloading equipment and crank out as many rounds as they can in the shortest time possible. After all, "time is money." This process gives rise to ammunition which is inconsistent, and once in a great while, even dangerous.

During the reloading process, if you leave out a primer or a bullet, there is no safety issue. The real problem is in the powder. The goal is obviously to put exactly the correct amount of powder into every case, every time. If you skip the powder altogether, the result will be a "squib load" where the bullet is propelled only by the primer. The bullet travels just a short distance down the barrel and stops. If another round is fired right behind it, disaster looms. If the powder charge is present but too small, a semi-auto weapon will likely malfunction because there was insufficient energy to run the action. If there is too much powder, the chamber pressure climbs right off the charts and the gun comes apart. This is the one you read about and see in YouTube videos. This is the one which sends people to the Emergency Room, or the mortuary.

In rifle ammunition, the powder charge nearly fills the entire space available inside the case. Thus, any extra powder quickly spills right out the top. Handgun ammo is different. The powder charge occupies only a small portion of the case and getting a "double charge" is quite easy. Double charging is pretty common because it merely requires that you get distracted and pull the handle of your reloader twice instead of once. The phone rings; pull twice. The dog wants out; pull twice. The opposing team scores a touchdown; damn it, pull twice.

Double powder charges blow up handguns. Here is what happens when you fire a double-charged load:

- The primer detonates as usual.
- The powder ignites as usual. However, there is so much powder that the resulting gasses cause tremendous, excessive pressures.
- The gas travels the path of least resistance. Normally, that path is down the barrel behind the bullet. However, in the case of a double charge, the bullet can't move down the barrel fast enough to accommodate all that gas.
- The path of least resistance is now right through the gun itself, and the gun blows apart.
- Depending on the type of weapon, the gasses may be directed down through the magazine well (common with semi-autos), or up through the top of the chamber (common with revolvers).
- Chunks of the gun are now flying through the air, and routinely into the shooter.
- Sometimes the gun is salvageable, sometimes not.
- Sometimes the shooter is salvageable, sometimes not.

Over the years, I have seen perhaps a dozen guns destroyed by double-charged ammo. In my college days, a penny-pinching friend of mine named Andy was sick of purchasing factory .45 ammo for his 1911. He shopped around for quite a while until he found a second-hand, very rudimentary reloader. No reloading manuals or chronographs for Andy; those things cost extra. As he experimented with various loads, Andy turned out a few double-charged rounds. I was with him on the range when one of those rounds made its way into the chamber. The first indication that things were amiss was the sound. The usual crack of the .45 was instead a distinct "boom." That was followed by him dropping the gun, hopping around clutching his hands, and lots of swearing. In this case the gun was salvaged. He needed new stocks and a replacement magazine.

A competitor friend of mine in Colorado named Phil recruited his daughter to help him reload .45 ammo. He was preparing for the Nationals match and was shooting more ammo than he could load. He owned top-of-the-line equipment and had reloaded for decades. This however, was the first time his daughter had ever tried it. Somewhere along the line, she pulled the handle twice. I happened to be on the range with Phil when he fired that round. The gun was a 1911 and the hot gasses went down the magazine well, as expected. As a bonus, the entire hood of the barrel (the part you see in the ejection port), broke clean off and shot back toward Phil's head. The chunk of steel just missed Phil's right eye and instead hit his ear muffs. The muffs shattered and fell to the ground. Then the obligatory swearing began.

Handgun ammo is not the only type subject to problems. Let me give you a shotgun example. My dad graduated from the University of Oklahoma a long time ago, probably before Oklahoma was even a state. To say that he is a fan of Sooner's football would be a gross understatement. He was also an avid bird hunter, mostly dove and quail. His favorite bird gun was an old .410 Winchester Model 42 pump. He shot it quite a bit and got pretty good. A friend of his convinced my dad to buy a reloader. This was billed as a win-win proposition. He could watch football <u>and</u> reload shotgun shells at the same time.

When teams like Notre Dame, Penn State, or Alabama were playing, quality control over the reloading process was pretty good. My dad was actually willing to occasionally look away from the game to check his work. When Oklahoma was playing, quality control went completely to shit! It was during those Oklahoma games that he produced some .410 shells which were just a bit too long. If you put those oversized shells into a modern shotgun, there would be no safety issue because the gun simply wouldn't fire. However, his Model 42 was pretty old. Even if the shell was not all the way into the chamber, you could still press the trigger. In that scenario, the brass portion of the shell would rupture and little shards of brass would be jetted out the bottom of the gun into your arm. I found this out the hard way.

We went as a family to the local range to shoot dad's Model 42. I was only eight years old and not very interested. Moreover, this particular gun was equipped with a 30-inch barrel and a ridiculously long stock. It was difficult for me to even hold this gun properly, let alone hit anything with it. Regardless, I was a good sport. My mom threw a clay pigeon into the air and I pressed the trigger. As predicted above, I got the blast of hot gas and metal in my arm and dropped the gun into the dirt. Both of my parents moved with cat-like reflexes; my mom toward my injured arm and my dad toward his Model 42!

I learned to hate reloads at an early age. Go Sooners!

These are the sorts of reasons we don't allow reloads at Front Sight, and you should steer clear of them. Factory ammunition is not perfect, obviously. However, I have never seen a factory load blow up a gun. I'm sure it has happened somewhere, but not during the millions of rounds I have seen fired over the last 25 years. Go home with the same number of eyes and fingers you arrived with - shoot factory ammunition.

Look at this silliness. Here I am; banana-backed, holding Dad's mile-long .410 shotgun, missing a front tooth, and more interested in the camera than the front sight!

CATEGORY X

IT seems I have a thousand little stories from almost 30 years in the firearms training industry. Every day it's something new. Let me tell you some of those stories using a very simple format. First, I'll list the general "category" the story fits into, like "Unbelievable Shots," "Weird," or "Little White Lie." Then I'll give the briefest of preambles and get right to the punch line. Life is short…eat dessert first!

Category: Poor Choice of Words. We had a husband and wife team in a 4-Day Defensive Handgun course back in 1999. I was on the line helping the wife with Type 1 Malfunction clearances. The proper procedure is Tap, Rack, and Flip. She was doing fairly well but she kept forgetting to Flip. I told her "Not much of a flip; although you have one hell of a rack."

Category: Vulnerable. After months of EMT training, we were finally certified and heading out to a celebration dinner. When we arrived at the restaurant, I stepped into a stall in the men's room. As I was undoing my belt and wrestling with my gear, my Glock 23 fell clean out of the holster. It hit the side of my shoe and went skidding into the next stall and came to rest between a pair of feet. Shit, this is quite a predicament. "Um, excuse me sir, could you please slide that gun back over this way?" All's well that ends well!

Category: Underwhelming. I hired a guy named Sven to assist in the Program Gun department of Front Sight. He was a First Family Member, had taken numerous courses, and had even attended Instructor Development. He had a very strong resume and interviewed really well. He lasted exactly four hours. He left for lunch and never came back. We called and called, and sent several e-mails over the next two days. We heard nothing from him until we sent him an e-mail informing him that if we don't hear back from him, we were going to file a missing persons report with the Nye County Sheriff. He casually replied that there was no need for that.

Category: New to the Game: In May of 2007, we had a lady in a handgun course who was learning about malfunctions for the first time. Upon hearing the term "out of battery," she asked the Range Master "Do I need to change the batteries in my gun?"

Category: Weird. We had a student leave his rifle on the range at the conclusion of his course. It was sitting right there in the rifle rack, all alone. Of course, I thought the student had simply forgotten it. Or maybe he left it there as a gratuity, as is common in Africa to give your gun to "Bwana," the great white hunter. We contacted this guy and he said that he just didn't want the rifle anymore. This has actually happened twice. Both times on the rifle range. Both times with nice guns. Come to think of it, both times with the same Range Master. Maybe I'm onto something here.

Category: Hidden Agenda. A few years back, I was forced to question the motives of a particular female student named Paula. She was an attractive lady in her mid-40's, well dressed, and drove a high-end BMW. Come to find out, she was a very successful attorney. I had just delivered the Loading and Unloading lecture in a 4-Day Defensive Handgun course when Paula raised her hand, but with a great deal of hesitation. She slowly and quietly asked if she should wear disposable latex gloves when loading her magazines when she gets back home. I immediately wondered why anyone would wear latex gloves when loading magazines. Prevent lead poisoning? Keep their hands clean and soft? I had to ask. She responded with several comments which I found alarming. "I carry a gun which cannot be traced back to me. I only carry ammunition which has already been chambered in several other guns. That way the scratches on the brass case are not unique to my weapon. And I wonder if fingerprints on the ammunition are erased by the heat when the weapon fires. Or should I wear gloves?" I simply asked "What are you planning?" She chuckled and said "Oh, no, I'm not planning anything. I just want to be sure that if I shoot someone and ditch the gun, nothing can be traced back to me." I responded with "What kind of attorney are you, anyway?"

Category: Undeserved Compliment. In the summer of 1987, I was teaching a handgun course at Gunsite. I was running one of the indoor simulators (i.e. shoot houses) and I had been there all morning. The problem was the restrooms were located at the other end of the property. Since I was between groups of students, I figured I had sufficient time to run behind one of the nearby cedar trees. I unbuckled my Milt Sparks leather belt which was tan in color and quite wide at 1¾". Midstream, literally, I heard a lady's voice gasp "Oh my!" I looked up and saw Elizabeth, a lovely middle-aged woman from Pennsylvania, staring at my midsection. From her perspective, my dangling belt looked anatomically correct, and quite complimentary! The instructor who was walking her to the simulator figured it out pretty quickly and said "No Elizabeth, that's his belt!"

Category: Bad Attitude. In 2003 I was running an Instructor Development course with about 25 candidates. One of the candidates was a young, hard-charging cop from Florida named Robert and he was easily the best shooter in the bunch. However, he strutted around like he was on stage. Clearly, this attitude wasn't going to cut it so I pulled him aside to deliver the bad news. He was shocked that he was getting cut and his surprise soon gave way to anger. I extended my hand and he actually bladed-off, as if to prepare for a gunfight. My fellow staff members saw this happen and swooped right in. I greatly enjoyed our strength in numbers.

Category: Letdowns. In September of 2011, we had a "garage sale" to rid ourselves of all the crap we had accumulated which we couldn't sell in the Pro Shop. We had an array of oddball stuff like a left-handed holsters for a Walther PPK and a sling swivel kit for a shotgun nobody had ever heard of. We priced this stuff cheap to sell fast, which was a better option than the trash can. On the "Odds & Ends" table were three adapters for some kind of rifle bipod. These retailed for $30 each and I had priced them at $2. The crowd was buzzing and it seemed that everyone wanted to have first crack at the random stuff we couldn't sell over the last decade. During the buzz, when nobody was looking, someone put all three of the bipod parts into a single bag and handed over two dollars. They placed the two empty bags back in just the right spot so as to appear unmolested. Now, who would rip off a couple of $30 parts when the price was only $2?

Category: Short Season. People occasionally ask me why we don't run courses at our facility in Alaska all year. A picture is worth a thousand words:

This is the very tip-top of my Ford Explorer which stands about six-feet tall. This photo was taken on March 28, 2012 after a bit of the snow had already melted.

<u>Category: Not Immune.</u> Sure, Front Sight is located in the Mojave Desert. But that doesn't mean we are exempt from snow. Those of you who braved the chill during the first week of January 2011, we salute you!

Range 1 (center) and the classroom (left) at Front Sight under a fresh blanket of Mojave Desert snow, January 3, 2011.

<u>Category: Lousy Lectures.</u> Naish was scheduled to deliver two lectures back-to-back. The First Family presentation was during lunch followed immediately by the Color Code of Mental Awareness and the Combat Mindset. At the conclusion of First Family, Naish got busy talking to a guy who was interested in the Front Sight development. Naish turned to me and said "Brad, you're on for the Color Code lecture." What the hell? I certainly knew the Color Code but had never lectured it. Naish said "Relax, you've seen me give it a hundred times. You will be fine." Boy, some consolation. I had also seen Joe Montana

throw a hundred touchdown passes, and Dan Rather deliver a hundred news broadcasts, and Mike Tyson pound a hundred guys into submission. I wasn't ready for any of those either! I was NOT prepared...and it showed. I completely left out Condition Black and the entire discussion about Combat Mindset. The only upside was these folks got that much more time on the range! What an embarrassment. If you were in that particular course back in 1999, I am still sorry!

Category: After Action Reports. Front Sight students are certainly under no obligation to report back to us if they get into a shooting after receiving training from us. Nonetheless, quite a few people have shared their experiences with me. Here is what I know to date:

- Eight people have let me know they were forced to use their weapon to stop an adversary. In each and every case, the outcome was perfect.
- Surely additional students have been in shootings, but I don't have that data.
- I know of no Front Sight student who was involved in a gunfight and lost.
- Perhaps 75-100 students have reported to me that they were able to avoid a gunfight by using the Color Code of Mental Awareness. That is the most satisfying statistic of all.

Category: Confusion. In January of 1997, we were running our very first submachine gun event. After all of the lectures, demonstrations, and dry practice, we had a gentleman shoot his first burst directly into the dirt in front of his feet. He never even bothered to point at the target.

Category: If at First You Don't Succeed. The rule is nobody ever passes the Handgun Combat Master test on their first try. I know a guy who took the test over 100 times before passing it. "Even a blind squirrel finds a nut sometimes." There is an exception to the above rule and that is Chuck Taylor. He indeed passed the test on his first crack and has passed it numerous times since. I once watched him pass it handily with a shameful, little double-action 9mm, from under concealment, in 30° weather. Chuck Taylor is one hell of a shooter.

Category: Misunderstanding. In June of 1998, I was briefing the students on the tactical simulator they were about to experience. I explained that the staff will be right behind them as they shoot at photographic targets. I told the students to look at the hands of the targets to determine if it is a threat. A lady raised her hand and said "I don't feel comfortable shooting the instructors." I responded "I don't either; I'm glad you asked!"

Category: Good Save. A lady was eating her lunch in the car on a calm, sunny day back in 2001. She had a serious almond allergy but loved sunflower seeds. You guessed it; her bag of sunflower seeds contained some crushed almonds. She was immediately in trouble and one of our staff called me on the radio. As EMT-B's we were not allowed to carry EpiPen auto-injectors. I did however, have some children's liquid Benadryl on hand. I managed to get as much down her throat as I did down her front. Five minutes later, she was happy again and finished the course in fine shape. (Shh…we now carry EpiPens.)

Category: Rule 1 (All Guns Are Always Loaded). In December of 1998, our instructor named Guy was working with the students in a 2-Day Defensive Handgun course. A gentleman turned around with a gun in his hand, finger on the trigger, and accidentally covered Guy and several fellow students. Guy quickly got him turned back down range. The student said "Don't worry, it's not loaded; see," as he pressed the trigger. The loud "bang" was all the reprimand that student needed.

Category: Poor Choice of Words. I was running a submachine gun course back in 1999 using the Cobray M-11's. That gun is equipped with a very unfriendly safety which can be difficult to operate. I unwittingly told the group "If you get a stiff one, reach around with your support hand and take care of it."

Category: Perilously Close to a Stupid Question. During my morning welcome lecture, I describe the amount of material we cover in the course by saying "We pack about 4½ to 5-days worth of material into a 4-day format…" A student named Jim raised his had and said that he is in a 2-Day course. I said "Okay, for you, we pack about 2½ to 3 days worth of material into a 2-Day format."

Category: Misspoken Words. In November of 2001, Range Master Chris Fisher had his 4-Day Handgun students up on the line for the next exercise. He intended to shout "The range is clear," and instead got "The range is queer!"

Category: Surely You Jest. In July of 2002, one of our Line Coaches asked me if there should be two participants in the Man-on-Man competition.

Category: Machismo B.S. I worked alongside a guy for a couple of years who was a cop in Southern California. He had been in a number of shootings, all of them deemed justifiable. After hours, he would get together with his law enforcement buddies, raise their glasses, and congratulate each other on how many people they had shot. He would even say "Shooting someone feels better than anything else I can think of. And I mean ANYTHING (wink, wink)." This mindset is complete bullshit and you shouldn't buy into it. The best gunfight is the one which never occurs, the one which you avoid because you were in Condition Yellow, and the one where you don't have to face any criminal and civil liability afterwards.

Category: Déjà Vu. In December of 2001, we had a student named Marv who was having some trouble getting the hang of it. Specifically, he would bend over on the line and cover his left arm with the muzzle. We reminded him "Don't bend over, and certainly don't cover yourself or anyone else with the muzzle." After Marv had done this twice, I stayed very close to him in hopes of preventing a third occurrence. Indeed, he did it again, too quickly for me to intervene. I said "Marv, you may not know it, but you just did it again." He was puzzled "What? I did this?"

as he demonstrated by pointing the muzzle of his loaded gun at his left arm. I said "Yep, just exactly like that. Have I told you about the huge benefits of dry practice? Let me introduce you to the red gun."

Category: Misspoken Words. In November of 2004, Naish was lecturing at lunch during a 4-Day Defensive Handgun course. He promised "Your gunhandling, your marksmanship, and your package will be the best it can be."

Category: New to the Game. Back in February of 2006, a 4-Day Defensive Handgun student said to the Range Master "I'm blind in one eye. Which eye do you propose I use for a proper sight picture?" The Range Master replied, "Your choice."

Category: Pretty in Pink. Right after lunch I stepped up to deliver my lecture on the Color Code of Mental Awareness and the Combat Mindset. As I delivered the lecture, I looked around the room making eye contact with as many students as possible. Sitting in the very front row was a young girl who was maybe 16 years old. She sat with her mom on one side, dad on the other. She was slouched down low in her chair which put her feet and legs well out in front of the narrow table. She wore a loose pair of pink short-shorts, with absolutely nothing underneath. She arranged everything for maximum visibility and it damn near derailed my lecture. From that moment on, I had to ignore her half of the room. That evening when Scott finished his lecture on Moral and Ethical Decisions, he came directly to me and said "You wouldn't believe what just happened." I said "Let me guess, pink short-shorts!"

Category: New to the Game: In November of 2007, we had a lady in the 4-Day Defensive Handgun course who was struggling to absorb the new terminology and techniques. Around mid-morning of day one, she asked "Shouldn't we slow down? We've only been here for three hours and already you are asking us to hold our magazines."

Category: <u>Perilously Close to a Stupid Question.</u> In March of 2011, we had just handed out the certificates at the end of a 4-Day course. One of the students walked up to his Range Master and asked "Where do you think I could score a bag of pot?" The Range Master said "You aren't likely to find any around here." We subsequently moved that student over to the "black list."

Category: <u>Undeserved Compliment.</u> In November of 2011, Molly took a 4-Day Defensive Handgun course. I spoke with her a couple weeks later and she said "You guys are real professionals…even in the awkward moments." I thanked her, of course, and then asked her "What awkward moments?" She explained how her shirt had come untucked and was at risk of getting tangled up with the gun inside the holster. Our very nice Line Coach named Steve tucked her shirt in for her while she held the gun. I knew she was just yanking my chain. Surely one of my guys had given her $10 to tell me that story. Not the case, she was sincere and complimentary. I had to humbly explain that Steve had gotten his duties completely backwards. <u>He</u> is supposed to hold the gun!

Category: <u>Don't Touch My Knob.</u> In the summer of 2005, I had a father and son team come to Front Sight Alaska for a Handgun Skill Builder course and then a day of fishing. The son, Bobby, was in his early 30's and was the most fidgety, twitchy person I have ever had in the boat. He touched and tinkered and fiddled with everything. He spun round-and-round in his seat and peeked inside the cooler every few minutes. He was a five-year-old boy trapped in a 30-year-old body. We were in the drift boat fishing the lower Kenai for kings. It was still early in the season and I knew the odds of success were slim. Regardless, I rowed like a slave all day. Very near the end of the trip, we lucked into a huge strike on Bobby's rod. The rod bent over in the rod holder to the point where the tip was in the water. The rod literally vibrated and hummed, but only for a second. In an instant, the rod shattered and the line went limp. Little did I know, somewhere along the line, Bobby had tightened the drag as hard as he possibly could, until the knob would turn no more.

Category: Can't Get it Out of My Head. In the spring of 2007, I was driving down Front Sight Road and noticed a small, two-man tent pitched off the road a ways. There seemed to be nobody around and no vehicle nearby. Campers are pretty common at Front Sight but only in the designated camping area. This tent was at least a mile down the road. I noticed all of this but I didn't stop. Later that morning, one of our staff called me on the radio and needed to talk to me immediately. He launched into a story about how he was driving down Front Sight Road, saw a tent, nobody around, etc. He stopped to check on the tent because the wind was kicking up and the zippered door was flapping in the breeze. When he walked up to the tent and looked inside, he was aghast to see two guys ...well...do you remember the movie *Brokeback Mountain*?

Category: Show of Support. We have lots of students who get vanity license plates reading FNTSITE or something similar. However, the most permanent show of support comes from Robert in Southern California. Robert got a really big tattoo of the Front Sight logo, complete with the text "Front Sight Firearms Training Institute" on the back of his calf, just below the knee. After hours, some of the staff made comments involving "Kool-Aid."

Category: One of the Best Shots Ever. In April of 1998 we were conducting training at a leased facility near Bakersfield called 5-Dogs Range. This facility wasn't stellar but it was sufficient for our needs at the time. Spring is a gorgeous time in this neck of the woods; the grass is lush and cute little ground squirrels are everywhere. Behind the backstop of the rifle range was a bluff standing maybe a hundred feet tall. Naish was standing under the shade structure when a squirrel stood up at the very edge of the bluff. Naish hauled out his .40-caliber Glock and pointed in. My mind raced to calculate the odds. Let's see; the shot is offhand, about 250 yards away, a target the size of a lemon, and 80-90 inches of bullet drop. I'd say the odds are one in 500 of getting a hit on the very first round. I'm glad I didn't take that bet! Naish was also smart enough to leave his gun holstered for the rest of the weekend because he knew he couldn't duplicate such a heroic shot!

The scene of the crime at 5-Dogs Range in Bakersfield, California. Naish shot an unsuspecting squirrel with his handgun as it peered innocently over the bluff in the background. April 1998.

<u>Category: Good Save.</u> I was on a pronghorn antelope hunt near Harlowton, Montana back in 1988. A group of folks I had met at the trap and skeet range in Missoula offered to take me hunting and I accepted. We met the night before the hunt at some restaurant/bar on the main drag in Harlowton. I ate and they drank. Come sunrise, I was a bit concerned about the blood alcohol content of my fellow hunters, but they seemed coherent enough. I was surprised at the number of women and children in the group, none of whom were at the restaurant the night before. We got into five different pickup trucks and drove to the first

hunting spot. Upon arrival, everyone quietly eased out of the trucks. We crawled on hands and knees for maybe 30 yards to the crest of a little rise only to see a nice herd of antelope already on the run. We dashed back to the trucks and piled in. The plan was to drive a couple of miles down the road to see if we could head them off, and hopefully get a shot. Since this jaunt was supposed to be short, I jumped into the bed of the truck instead of the cab. Driving the truck was Guy, in the passenger seat was his wife, and in the middle was their two-year-old son in a car seat. Guy put his 7mm Remington Magnum in the rifle rack of the back window, which was slid open. I was standing in the bed, leaning against the cab, so Guy's rifle was just in front of my thighs. As we drove the short distance, I noticed Junior's hands fiddling with the rifle over his head. Junior's fingers were all over the trigger and the muzzle was mere inches from mom's head. The hair on the back of my neck stood up and I quickly reached in through the window and opened the bolt. Sure enough, the safety was off and there was a round in the chamber. It's possible that Junior could have messed with that trigger all day long with no ill effect. It's also possible that I just saved mom's life.

Category: Condition White. During a course back in October of 1996, on two consecutive days, Glock handguns were left sitting in bathroom stalls in the men's room. This tends to be a bit embarrassing for students, especially when we work so hard to instill proper gunhandling. However, the offenders here were not students. No, no. The first was a seasoned instructor, in fact a 4-Weapons Combat Master, and he received a blistering reprimand for his oversight from the Director of Curriculum at the time. The very next day it was the Director of Curriculum himself who left the restroom with an empty holster. The gun was recovered by a student who delivered it to Naish.

- Roll of toilet paper…$1
- Box of ammo…$20
- The body language and facial expression on the Director of Curriculum when Naish personally returned the wayward Glock…Priceless!

The Front Sight careers for both of these jokers sputtered to a halt shortly after this incident.

Category: Satisfying Handshake. My mom joined me at one of the handgun courses I took in the early days at Gunsite. As part of the training, the students went through an outdoor simulator called the West Wash. I went first, and then my mom. When she came out, I asked "Wasn't that great?" She was pretty stoic and rigid; not at all the reaction I expected. She was smart and told me her story only <u>after</u> we got back home. Gene, the instructor in the West Wash, spent the entire time hitting on my mom and nudging her through the exercise by grabbing her ass. In November of 2011, we had a guy show up at Front Sight for Instructor Development who looked familiar but I couldn't place him. Once I heard his self introduction, it all made sense. I walked right up to Gene and introduced myself with a hearty handshake. I didn't say a word about the incident from 25 years ago but apparently I didn't need to. At lunch on that very first day, he bowed out of the program. Seems he was smarter than I thought!

Category: Little Misunderstanding. Chaplain Dave took the 4-Day Defensive Handgun course back in April of 2011. He very much enjoyed the training but had one scathing comment:

> On day two during the lecture on "Color Code of Mental of Awareness" the instructor was making the point that just about anything can be used as a weapon...even a rolled up newspaper. He went on to say "A newspaper can be used for more than what you see in the porn movies (big smile)... Oh, I see you've watched some of those movies just like me!"

> I have to say, I was appalled that one of your instructors would make a comment like that with women and children present. I will not bring others nor recommend your organization when there is such blatant disregard for moral decency.

I asked Scott to please speak s-l-o-w-l-y and clearly when he describes how Jason Bourne, in the movie <u>Bourne Identity</u>, uses improvised weapons like ball point pens and rolled up newspapers!

<u>Category: Satisfying Snub.</u> Back in August of 1990, I was at Gunsite teaching a handgun course. I had driven up from Phoenix with three other instructors. We stopped in Chino Valley to see Lewey Awerbuck who was one of the full-time Range Masters at the time. We walked single-file into Lewey's meager little apartment and I was the last in line. Lewey shook the hand of each instructor ahead of me. As I stepped into the doorway, I too extended my hand. Lewey looked me right in the eye and left his hands down at his side. I have no idea why he disliked me so intensely, but he certainly did. In January of 2005, I was attending the SHOT show which is a big trade show in Las Vegas for the shooting and hunting sports. I was standing in one of the aisles talking to a couple of notable folks when Lewey approached. He strolled up with his cocky, life-of-the-party swagger and extended his hand to me. I looked right at him and kept my hands down at my side. I am not generally a grudge-holder, but there was significant satisfaction in returning the favor, even 15 years after the fact.

<u>Category: Bounty Hunter.</u> Back in the day, Jeff and Janelle Cooper had two house cats. One was a petite little thing and the other more robust and outdoorsy. A feral tomcat wandered onto the ranch and tangled with the smaller of the Coopers' cats. The feral tomcat won handily leaving behind only some fur and unidentifiable red chunks. Jeff was livid and put the word out to the staff to kill that "goddamned tomcat." As the maintenance guru Rich was headed out that evening, he saw a pair of eyes peering at him from up in the tree. Rich quickly loaded some birdshot into his shotgun and blew the little bastard right out of the tree. He marched over to the Coopers' house with the corpse to spread the good cheer and collect his brownie points. Janelle broke down at the sight of her second dead cat in 24 hours!

<u>Category: Didn't Think This Through.</u> We use tens of thousands of targets each year at Front Sight. And then there are the staples and the man-hours required to hang all those targets. We had a student in 2003 who offered up an easier way; "Why don't you get your targets printed in a stack and then bound at the top like a legal pad, or Big Chief tablet? Then you can hang the entire bundle at one time. When the top target is all shot-up, simply peel it off and expose a fresh target underneath." Hmm.

<u>Category: Above the Rules.</u> You know the Four Universal Firearms Safety Rules.
1. Treat every weapon as if it were loaded.
2. Never let the muzzle cover anything you are not willing to destroy.
3. Keep your finger off the trigger until you are ready to shoot.
4. Be sure of your target, and what's in line with your target.

Those succinctly sum up firearms safety. They don't address training at all, but they completely handle safety. They were created by Jeff Cooper back in the late-'70's and they remain intact today. One of Jeff's top Range Masters went out on his own after a long stint at Gunsite. This guy focused mostly on shotgun training. He adopted a cute little range exercise to verify that his students had proper alignment between the firing side eye, the rear sight, and the front sight. He would have his students point their unloaded shotguns downrange and line up the sights. Then he would walk in front of the line, looking back at the shooters with his eye directly in front of the muzzle. If he saw proper alignment between the front sight, the rear sight, and the shooters eye, he could assume the shooter had it correct. He walked the entire line placing his head in front of every single 12-gauge shotgun. As Front Sight staff, we have all been covered by God-knows-how-many muzzles. And each time was <u>unintentional</u>.

<u>Category: Full of Hot Air.</u> Y2K was a complete joke. But nobody knew for sure that it was going to be a joke until Y2K + 1 day. For months, we listened to people talk about impending

Armageddon, food shortages, no electricity, and the fall of society. Better stock up now on water, food, guns, ammo, generators, fuel, gold, short-wave radios, batteries, medicine, etc. I never thought we were in peril, not for one second. However, I was still pretty nervous when Y2K rolled around, but for a completely different reason. In late-1999, Front Sight was still in the process of building the main classroom, Pro Shop, and armory. We had no gun storage on-site. Therefore, every Front Sight gun, including every Uzi, M-16, and M-11, was stored in safes at my house. I knew that when the clock struck 12, every cop in Las Vegas would be busy down on the Strip. What better time to kick in Brad's door, put a gun to his empty head, and abscond with hundreds of full-auto weapons? My wife wasn't impressed by this theory in the least. At around 10:00 she simply said "Good luck," and went to bed. Apparently, this battle was going to fall squarely on the shoulders of me and my daughter. At around 12:45, my daughter and I quit looking at the front door and also went to bed.

Category: E-Mail Snafu. We had a rifle instructor named Paul who we hired-out as a technical advisor to a movie production company in Canada. Paul was a good choice for the project because he would make a capable technical advisor and I could live without him in Nevada. He was on the movie set for a couple of months and continuously called to tell me how he was overworked and underpaid. I told him I would get his expenses covered as soon as he sent me some receipts. He took to e-mailing me his receipts one at time. Breakfast $10.25. Stamps $2.65. Gas $47.13. Somewhere in this e-mail campaign, Paul got all screwed up. Instead of receipts, he started attaching photographs. The first one I opened featured a girl; maybe 20 years old, topless, and covered below the waist only by a souvenir Canadian flag with the maple leaf where the fig leaf usually resides. Then a few more receipts. Dinner $27.45. Gloves $17.59. Then a photo of a different girl, this time completely naked and with Paul at her side. I called Paul and asked "Hey, how's it going up there?" He replied "Oh, man, it's rough, I am working all hours of the day and night, not getting much sleep, but the people are really friendly up here." I came down like a ton of bricks and cut Paul right there. As far as I know, he is still up there chasing that Canadian maple leaf.

Category: Confusing Lingo. We had a student come into the Pro Shop in need of .270 rifle ammunition. We had two choices; .270 Winchester and .270 Weatherby. He said "No, no, no. I need .270 Winonly." I told him "No such thing as Winonly." He was adamant, and a little sassy, if I do say so. He asserted bluntly "It says right on the rifle, .270 Winonly." I asked him to bring the rifle in, which he did. I pointed to the engraving on the barrel, ".270 Win. Only." That means ".270 Winchester Only," and we have that right over here.

Category: Above the Fray. It's a lot of work being on the range all day. Your feet hurt, your back aches, it's hot, it's cold, etc. Unfortunately, that's the nature of the job. A couple of Front Sight staff members recently attended a course at another school under a well-known instructor. They returned with quite a story. It seems this "instructor" found some solutions to standing on the range all day. Solution #1: Have someone else run the range. However, that option was not always available. Solution #2: Sit, relax, and run the range from your posterior. If the weather was nice, this guy would unfold a large, comfortable, camp chair; the kind with the drink holder integrated into the armrest. He would set it up behind the line a ways, open a bottle of Snapple iced tea, and run the range. If the weather was hot or cold or windy, or there was a good football game on the radio, he would sit in his vehicle. He would park his car on the range so the driver's side window faced the students, turn on the heater or air conditioner as appropriate, and bark out the commands. A true professional. Maybe this is something we can teach in the Instructor Development course.

Category: Dearly Beloved. Back in 2001, we had two Front Sight students who were seeking a unique venue for their wedding. They called Naish and solicited his permission to hold the ceremony at Front Sight. We were delighted to host the wedding and we did so during a regular 4-Day Defensive Handgun course. In keeping with the theme, instead of trading rings, husband and wife traded Beretta 9mm handguns! This wouldn't be my ideal arrangement but it was pretty darn fun to be part of.

Category: Very Important Question. Back in 2010 I was lecturing the Color Code of Mental Awareness to a group of about 400 students. I was about at the midway point when a student named George stood up from his chair and walked down the aisle toward the front of the classroom. He never broke stride and stepped right up on stage with me. I had no idea what he wanted, but I knew it must be serious. My mind raced to guess what it was; maybe he was sick or maybe he had to leave and wanted someone to know. I neglected to turn my microphone off so everyone in the room was privy to George's question. He slowly, methodically told me "I have recently started shooting a Glock. I find the magazine release difficult to use. Do you have any suggestions on how to better press the magazine release? Or maybe there is a replacement, aftermarket version available?" I asked George if maybe we could talk about this after the lecture. He agreed and went back to his seat. Wow, that was odd. Now, where the hell was I?

Category: Funny Question. In July of 2004 we had a German family in a 4-Day Defensive Handgun course in Alaska. These folks had only a modest command of the English language. The matriarch of the family asked, "If I give boom-boom to him while he is giving boom-boom to me, will he die?" She meant "shooting" of course, but I had to giggle.

Category: Learn to Keep My Mouth Shut. We were hosting the World SWAT Challenge at Front Sight back in March of 2005. As part of the setup, we placed some steel rifle targets way out yonder, at about 500 yards. Steve, one of our Range Masters, wondered out loud about the odds of hitting that far target with his Glock 23. I blurted out "Hell, if you hit that target with the first round, I'll give you $500." What an idiot I was. And I even consider myself to be a reasonably intelligent guy.

Category: Who Said? "Jack" has been in the firearms training industry a good while longer than I. Over the years, he found that most people wanted to train from March through August. Earlier than March is hampered by weather, depending of course on where you live. Later than August is hampered by family vacations, the kids going back to school, tight budgets after the summer months, and the holidays. Jack went so far as to say "You can't train anybody after Labor Day." Wow, little did we know! I started wondering just how many people we have trained "after Labor Day." So, I picked one weekend, the first weekend in November, and looked back at enrollment over the last five years. Here are the stats:

First weekend in November 2008 = 551 students on-site
First weekend in November 2009 = 685 students on-site
First weekend in November 2010 = 840 students on-site
First weekend in November 2011 = 909 students on-site
First weekend in November 2012 = 1,135 students on-site

The month of November is no anomaly. Front Sight now trains hundreds of students EVERY weekend of the year. There are lots of naysayers out there. Listen to them at your own peril.

Category: Having a Bad Day. In February of 2012, we had a lady named Joni in the Instructor Development course. One of the very first exercises we do in that course is shoot a very simple skills test. That gives us a peek at the participants' baseline shooting skills. Joni was shooting a basic S&W double-action 9mm but she couldn't even get it loaded. We let her struggle with it for a while and then helped her get a round into the chamber. She went on to do VERY poorly in the skills test and we dismissed her from the course right then before anyone got hurt! Before departing, she told the staff "I am actually a very good shooter. I teach the Israeli's how to shoot Uzi's. I'm just a little off my game today."

Category: Speech Impediment. When I was in the 7th grade, I took a "speech" class, which I honestly thought was a class for kids with speech impediments. Since I didn't have a speech impediment, I figured this was going to be easy. Then...what the hell…I have to get up in front of the group and deliver a speech? That's the moment I learned just what stage fright was. On occasion, I still get a little nervous before I take the stage, but not like in Mrs. Wilder's class!

Brad Ackman lecturing to a group of handgun students, February 2009.

Category: Poor Choice of Words. Richard, one of our Range Masters was talking to the 4-Day Handgun students about watching the hands of your opponent to identify a weapon. He said "If you are confronted by a guy pulling a python out of his pants…" Of course, he meant a Colt Python .357!

Category: Advice for Boys. I once listened to a scholarly old gentleman pontificate about what boys should learn on their journey toward manhood. The list included some very lofty things such as learn to speak Latin and old English, read the Bible and the Koran, fully understand every word in *The Odyssey* and *The Iliad*, swim the Nile, climb the pyramids, and walk on the moon! Okay, my advice is far simpler. Give Junior an air compressor, a Dremel tool, and a crappy old 1911 that you can live without. In a month's time, the 1911 will be scrap but Junior will be well versed in metallurgy, the operation of firearms, working with his hands, and the difference between "just a little" and "way too much."

Category: 3-Dimensional Thinking. In April of 2011, I held a staff meeting with all the instructors and the maintenance crew the day before an Advanced Tactics course. We discussed a variety of things including the layout of the simulator bays, timing for the night shoot, staffing, and other logistics. After an hour or so, everyone had a thorough understanding of the game plan and we got to work. At the end of the day, I checked all the simulators. They all looked perfect with the exception of one, which wasn't yet done. The maintenance guys planned to finish it in the morning before the students arrived. That particular scenario was a vehicle stage where the student shoots a variety of photographic targets through the open car window while in the driver's seat. And that's what the maintenance guys set up. But they neglected to move the huge, metal, job box which holds the spare targets, tape, and spray paint. That box was <u>directly downrange</u> from one of the targets. How the maintenance guys overlooked that, I'll never know. How the instructor running the scenario missed it is baffling also. After 100+ students shot that scenario, the job box was reduced to Swiss cheese. Every single target, every roll of tape, and every can of spray paint was completely destroyed. Oh, but look at all the pretty colors inside the box from those paint cans!

Category: Mirror Image. In June of 1997, we had an officer from the California Highway Patrol who was having difficulty qualifying with his handgun. He sought out some additional training, which is how we were introduced to him. I noticed a little problem on the very first morning of the course during practice of loading and unloading. To unload, this gentleman placed the muzzle of his <u>loaded</u> handgun against his sternum to better hold the gun steady while he worked on it. I immediately intervened with "Keep the muzzle pointed down range." Like a ballerina, he spun 180°, so the muzzle was indeed pointed down range...and still right into his chest!

Category: Helping Hand. One evening in March of 1998, I had just finished setting up the ranges at our leased facility in Bakersfield, California. I was driving back to the Holiday Inn Express and noticed a car off the side of the road, apparently stuck in the mud. A lady was pacing around looking quite distraught. Like the true gentleman that I am, I pulled over and asked how I could help. She informed me that she had run out of gas, and then while pushing her car to the shoulder, she rolled the car right over her foot. I gave her a ride to the gas station and we filled up a 5-gallon gas can. After I poured the gas into her car, she shook my hand and gave me a $5 bill for my troubles. Then she asked "What hotel are you staying at so I can come over later and thank you properly?" I told her "I'm staying at the, umm, the Best Western. Yeah, that's it." She smiled, got into her car, and then absolutely floored the accelerator. She shot mud all over me and my vehicle. She made it about 100 yards and careened over the embankment at Bear Mountain and Highway 99. Her vehicle was high-centered which prevented her from falling the 30-feet or so to the highway below. The headlights pointed straight down, and the taillights pointed straight up. I guess she was pretty excited to get to the Best Western! Again the consummate gentleman, I pulled in behind her. She was sitting behind the wheel, bug-eyed, running the transmission through the gears while the engine was revved to the red line. I helped her out of the car and she was on the edge of a nervous breakdown. As she got out of the car, she locked the keys inside. California Highway Patrol happened onto the scene almost immediately. Her first comment to the cop was "Hi officer, I have only had two beers, honest."

Category: All Dressed Up. I was recently given a hardcover book which sported a very nice dust cover. On the inside back flap was a flattering photo of the female author. The photo was clearly a studio shot and not a hair was out of place. Below the image were credits for makeup, hair, and wardrobe. I laughed as I envisioned how that would play-out in my book:

- Makeup by "Mojave Desert Makeup," featuring their latest line called *Maximum UV Damage* to accentuate wrinkles and age spots.
- Hair by "Salt and Pepper Men's Salon" celebrating this season's trend toward both graying <u>and</u> thinning.
- Wardrobe by "Nazi Boy Scout Uniforms" presenting this fall's *Black and Gray* collection in the always popular 50/50 cotton/poly blend.

<u>Category: Jurassic Park.</u> Back in 2002 and 2003, we ran a course called Hunter's Rifle. This was obviously a rifle course geared toward preparing the student for hunting, instead of self defense. This was a wonderful course which covered topics like weapon selection, bullet design, anatomy and shot placement, improvised field positions, use of shooting slings, range estimation, and care for the meat once the animal was down. To prepare for this course, we needed new steel targets which represented deer, elk, and antelope, instead of gang bangers. Additionally, we were destined to see rifle calibers like 7mm Remington Magnum and 300 Weatherby Magnum. Therefore, the targets needed to be robust enough to withstand that kind of severe punishment. We decided to have Kirk Reinschmidt of Hind Sight Targets build us a dozen animal targets out of 1-inch armor plate. This was going to be a spendy proposition! One of our former Range Masters was in charge of approving the designs before Kirk cut even a single inch of that wildly expensive steel. Our <u>former</u> Range Master gave the plans only a cursory glance and approved them. What we ended up with were whitetail deer the size of moose, and moose the size of Mack trucks! What a joke. I have seen Naish mad on more than one occasion, but this one was a doozy. The heart/lung area on some of these behemoths was the size of a refrigerator. The students loved the targets because they were so easy to hit. Shooting these targets was like shooting wooly mammoths in the Pleistocene or dinosaurs in the Jurassic. And that's the name that stuck. The canyon where we placed these targets is now affectionately known as "Jurassic Park."

What would be the appropriate caliber for a 2,000-pound mule deer?

Category: From Beyond the Grave. I am writing these words from beyond the grave, at least according to an internet rumor of a few years ago. Apparently I was killed on the handgun range by a student's negligent discharge. I consider this to be one hell of a promotion! My very existence has been elevated to the ranks of the "second shooter on the grassy knoll" and "President Bush orchestrated the events of 9/11!"

BIG-TIME INTERVIEW

In May of 2001, I was asked by one of our instructors named Dave if I would be willing to take part in a big-time radio interview. I had done countless lectures in front of large audiences and had been in front of the cameras on numerous occasions. But I had never done a radio interview before, let alone one which was billed as "big-time." Before I agreed, I asked a few questions. Basically, I wanted to make sure I was going into a gun-friendly venue. I also wanted the interview to focus on Front Sight, our students, and our training. I did not want to debate the various interpretations of the Second Amendment or get bogged down in a discussion about gun laws. Additionally, I did not want to have the callers haranguing me with some anti-gun agenda. "Oh, don't worry, we don't take any callers. It will just be you and me," Dave said. Sounded fine, so I agreed.

I drove to Front Sight and met Dave at the appointed time. From there, I followed him in my vehicle to Pahrump. Dave turned off on a lonely gravel trail, not even a proper road. After a mile or so of seeing absolutely nothing, I began to get an unsettled feeling and I had random thoughts about Ted Kaczynski and the like. Eventually, I saw a single-wide trailer way out in the distance with a massive antenna poking out of the top. This was definitely not what I expected, but then again, I had never done a radio interview before.

I got out of my car but Dave had already stepped inside. I had no idea what I was getting into and part of me wanted to get back in the car. My confidence was bolstered by the fact that I was wearing a gun, so I went inside. Dave introduced me to a guy who was clearly the technical end of this operation. I forget his proper name but Dave referred to him as the "Technician Magician." The single-wide trailer was divided in half by a wall which contained a sizeable glass window. One half of the trailer contained all the wires, switches, and knobs for the Technician Magician and the other half contained a table, a few chairs, and some microphones for Dave and me. The Magician hollered out "Two minutes!" and Dave gestured to my seat. Shit, so much for a little warm-up.

As cheesy as this deal seemed, I was still a little nervous because I really wanted to do well. I wanted to sound intelligent, and approachable, and say something useful. The Magician banged on the window and counted down with his fingers; Three, Two, One. Then he pointed through the glass as if to say "You're on!" Dave spoke into the microphone "Okay, well, umm, this is Dave and thanks for joining us for another half hour of Gun Talk. Today with me is, umm, Brad Ackman, Operations Manager of uh, Front Sight." Wow, I guess the pressure is off for sounding intelligent.

Dave and I talked shop for a few minutes and then Dave looked at the Magician through the glass. The Magician held up his hand making the sign of an "O," like a zero. Dave looked back to me so I assumed the "O" was a good thing. Perhaps it meant "zero problems...all is well...you guys are kicking ass!" Another 10 minutes or so passed when the Magician literally banged on the glass. Startled, Dave and I looked at the Magician who was holding up one finger and shaking it with enthusiasm.

We wrapped up the world's most plebian radio interview and shut off the microphones. This interview was such a joke that I was actually a touch embarrassed to be part of it. Dave and I stepped over to the Magician's half of the trailer. I asked the Magician what the hand signals of "O" and "1" meant. He referred me to a computer monitor. He said, "Well, since we are an INTERNET radio station, I can track how many people are listening at any given moment. For a long time we had nobody. But then we had somebody log in." I was shocked, "You mean we had only ONE guy listening to us?" Dave actually said to me "No, no…he probably had someone else in the room with him."

Hell, I should have turned around when I had thoughts of Ted Kaczynski.

EVOLUTION OF A LUNCH

REMEMBER how easy lunch was back in elementary school? Mom either made it for you or gave you money. It was never an issue. After that, lunch started to become a bigger deal. In high school, lunch involved a few buddies, a car, and a drive to Taco Bell. And you had better be back before the next period. In college, lunch was either about a girl or last-minute cramming for an exam (because you were out late last night with a girl). Once you hit corporate America, lunch took on a whole new meaning and became a venue for meetings, negotiations, and putting on airs. Hell, sometimes "lunch" lasted all afternoon and didn't even involve food!

At Front Sight, lunch has similarly evolved over the years. Well, without Taco Bell...or the girls...or the exams.

Back in April of 1996, Front Sight opened for business and we offered our courses in Bakersfield, California. Student enrollment was quite modest and the number of instructors on any given weekend was maybe five or six guys. Part of my early-morning ritual back then was to purchase lunch for the instructors at the Safeway deli. I soon knew exactly what everyone wanted. Naish liked roast beef and Swiss on wheat, yes on mayonnaise, no on mustard. A bag of Lay's Classic potato chips and two of those ghastly Lipton Brisk iced teas. Don wanted smoked turkey and cheddar on white, lettuce, mustard, hold the mayo. A small tub of macaroni salad and a diet Coke. And so it went. I even asked the folks at the deli counter to assemble the lunches in individual bags, complete with names (just like mom used to do). Total bill: $55-60.

That approach didn't last long. Our student numbers grew rapidly, and so did the number of hungry instructors at lunchtime. It was taking me way too long each morning to order individual sandwiches with custom condiments. I still shopped every morning at Safeway but I had to switch to purchasing bulk supplies. "Sorry guys, you will have to assemble your own sandwiches. And go wash your hands first." The instructors obviously preferred the old way of custom orders but they understood; this was progress, after all. The bulk supply approach was certainly appreciated by the maintenance staff because they took home any uneaten portions at the end of the course. Everyone was happy.

I distinctly recall one lunch break in Bakersfield. It was mid-September and the air was humid, stagnant, and hot. But, as a little pick-me-up for the staff, I had purchased a case of Henry Weinhard's root beer. First thing that morning, I put the bottles in a cooler, covered them with ice, and moved the whole shootin'-match out of sight. After everyone finished eating, I unveiled the cold bottles. Funny, you don't have to perform to a very high standard to be considered heroic when it's that hot outside. There we were; kickin' back in the shade, feet propped up, talking shop, and sipping from dark-amber, long-neck bottles. Naish walked by and literally came uncorked. He lambasted us with comments like "perception," "assumptions," "redneck shooting school," and "unprofessional." It was a low moment indeed to pour out those bottles!

When we got to Nevada in early-1999, we had instructors everywhere and I had to bow out of the lunch game. I hired a shopper/expediter and he became the lunch guru. He would take his pickup truck to Costco in Las Vegas and fill four huge coolers with food and ice. $750 later, we had lunches for the weekend.

The Costco approach was our routine for years. The only variable was the scale. As we started running courses every weekend, and we had 60 or more instructors on-site, the lunch bill would routinely hit $5,000 per month.

In January of 2011, we broke through yet another growth barrier at Front Sight. Instead of training only on weekends, we added midweek courses as well. This meant we were literally cramming eight days of training (a pair of four-day courses) into a seven day week. We significantly increased our staff numbers to support the huge jump in students. We also had to rethink our lunch routine. There was now a ton of staff to feed and we were running short on refrigerators, tables, chairs, and shade. To solve the problem, we switched from bulk supplies to catered meals. Beach Café came on board with us as a provider of boxed lunches for our students. As part of that arrangement, Beach Café also fed the staff. We still had to build additional seating, but we no longer made the huge Costco runs. At lunchtime, the instructors now leave the range, stroll into the lunch room, and relax. This is the new norm and it's infinitely better. As much as some may want to, there is no going back.

TRESPASSERS

WHEN my dad first took me dove hunting in eastern Colorado nearly 40 years ago, he had a couple of "hot spots" he wanted to try. The drive from Denver seemed eternal, especially with my dad at the helm. Entertaining the kids was not his forte, or even on his list of responsibilities. We turned off the highway and traveled untold miles down a gravel county road. From the gravel we made another turn, this time onto a narrower, dustier, dirt road. Then my dad pulled the family station wagon off the road and stopped. The nose of the car was facing a three-strand barbed wire fence. Beyond the fence were a couple of tire tracks imprinted vaguely on the rough prairie. This was crappy-looking land; certainly not wheat or corn country. It wasn't even proper cattle country. Bare, exposed soil was the norm with sparse patches of sage brush and a few clumps of wild grass which has long since succumbed to the summer heat. I found out later that my dad knew this place because he had drilled a couple of oil wells in this area a few years earlier. My dad told me to get out and open that gate. "What gate?" I was looking at a barbed wire fence. I saw no gate, and I saw even less reason to venture out onto that prairie. My dad was forced to put the car in park and get out and show me the redneck-rigging that passed for a gate. I knew I was lucky to be getting a personal tutorial. If the Oklahoma-Nebraska football game had already started, God himself couldn't budge my old man from behind the wheel because he would then be out of earshot of the radio.

I pulled the "gate" to one side and my dad drove through. I laid the tangle of wire on the ground and made my way back to the car. Before I even got to the door, my dad's head popped up over the top of the car. "What the hell are you doing?" Good question, I thought. I am out here touring Hades with my dad, listening to the Sooner's pre-game radio show, and now I am apparently going to get my ass chewed.

My dad laid out "gate etiquette" for me in stern detail. He was serious about this and I was a bit surprised. His lecture was less about cows and cars and more about philosophy and respect. "That gate is like the front door to someone's home. Would you enter without invitation? Would you force it open? Would you leave it open behind you?" All these ideas were new to me but I saw the logic in his discussion. I immediately adopted my dad's mindset on the issue. And that was my introduction to gates.

So, with that preamble, it fills me with curiosity and disgust that so many people have no respect for gates. Or fences, or signs for that matter. At Front Sight, we have had a few problems with trespassers over the years, both in Nevada and Alaska. We haven't had tons of problems, mind you, but a few. I think someone would have to be brazen right off the charts to illegally enter our firearms training facility and stay for very long!

We purchased our facility in Alaska from a local guy named Milhous who was a real piece of work (just like that bum Richard Milhous Nixon). Milhous had absolutely no understanding of personal property, pride of ownership, or quality workmanship. Everything in Milhous' life seemed to be communal property and therefore not worthy of much effort and attention. His truck was complete junk, almost as bad as some of the Front Sight range trucks! His tools were rusty, mixed up, and tossed into 5-gallon buckets. Similarly, he didn't care in the least if people stomped all over his land. People crossed his land on foot, dirt bikes, four-wheelers, and snowmachines. Milhous didn't mind; come one - come all. Well, that was the precedent, and I had to deal with it.

At the start of our very first summer season back in 2004, I installed a robust steel gate across our driveway. Then I put up a big, bold sign which warned "No Trespassing, Alaska Statutes…" We had so many people ignore that sign and stroll right in that I began to wonder if these folks could even read.

Here are a few examples of the trespassers we encountered that first year.

- A mother and her two daughters, all on horses, rode through the trees to get around the gate and then strolled up to the house to see if anyone was home.

- A 15-year-old girl on a four-wheeler rode through the woods and onto the vacant handgun range. I knew she was there by the screaming of the two-stroke engine as she carved "donuts" into the gravel. I ran to the range with a Benelli shotgun slung over my shoulder. I stepped directly in her path and she stopped. We traded a few words and she concluded with "F*** you old man!" She gave me the finger, laid into the throttle, and showered me with gravel. Then I watched her leave our property and pull into her own driveway just a few hundred yards down the road! I later enjoyed a hearty talk with her parents and an Alaska State Trooper friend of mine.

- An irate lady from down the street came waddling under the gate after hearing gunfire on the range. She was screaming at the top of her miserable lungs about bullets "Zinging over my roof!" I asked her if she lived in the house directly north of our facility and she concurred. Then I gestured to the orientation of the range, which faces due south. "I don't care about that, I am calling the Troopers!" When my Trooper friend arrived, he asked her bluntly "Why did you walk right past that No Trespassing sign?"

- A barefoot 40-year-old man strumming a guitar and singing to himself ducked under the gate and walked down to the house to see "What's goin' on?"

- An older gentleman had apparently parked at the gate and walked the quarter mile down to the house. I only knew of his presence when he knocked on the door. He informed me that in years past, Milhous would let him churn his enormous track dozer across our property as a short cut to land on the other side. The shortcut would eliminate the need for putting his dozer on a trailer and driving it on the streets. It was nice of him to ask, but the answer was "Hell no!" He was so sure the answer was going to be "Yes" that he had already staged the dozer at the front gate.

- Three guys on snowmachines crossed the frozen lake in February. They got off the snowmachines and were walking around the house, apparently looking for a way to break in. In the blink of an eye, they were staring down the muzzle of a state-issued M-16. They didn't realize that I have an Alaska State Trooper living on-site during the off-season. Such satisfaction!

The "No Trespassing" sign at our facility in Alaska which was ignored by so many people during our first year of operation back in 2004.

Front Sight Nevada is a remarkable piece of real estate. It is 550 contiguous acres surrounded 360° by federal land controlled by the Bureau of Land Management (BLM). That means encroachment is impossible, and we will forever be a private "island." Even with this degree of isolation, we have had a few minor trespassing issues over the years.

BLM land is open to off-road vehicles like four-wheelers and dirt bikes <u>as long as they stay on the designated trails</u>, which they never do. To ward off potential dirt bikers, we posted signs along the perimeter of the property declaring "No Trespassing, Warning, Live-Fire, Doom-and-Gloom, Blood-and-Guts, and Armageddon". Posting your property is a funny thing, though. Signs only work if the would-be trespasser has the ability to read, understands the content, and then gives a damn. You know the old saying about signs and padlocks keeping the honest people honest.

Generally, the dirt biker sees the warning signs and heads off in some other direction. If the rider ignores the signs and enters the property, the situation is nipped in the bud almost immediately, thanks to our on-site security staff. When the unmistakable whine and snap of a two-stroke dirt bike approaches, we dispatch a couple of our security guys to check it out. This has <u>always</u> been a peaceful, respectful affair. Now really, who would argue with the likes of Front Sight's security staff?

And then there was one particularly energetic idiot who must have just watched the old dirt bike classic *On Any Sunday*. He screamed right past the warning signs at the edge of the property and was headed toward the ranges. Imagine the scene...it's a calm sunny morning on the Rifle Range, students are at the 25-yard line, guns are loaded, Scott Hoerner is hollering the range commands "Line is Set...Ready..." Just then Evel Knievel appears midair, 15-feet over the steel targets, engine screaming, flying directly toward the students!

Scott is one cool customer. No shots fired. No injuries. No arrests. Funny, we haven't seen that particular dirt biker since.

No Trespassing Signs; when they don't work, we call it a "Failure to Stop!"

LIVE VICARIOUSLY

THE world of firearms training is literally built upon the graves of the good men and women who died because of the crappy training they received. We at Front Sight are humbled and very fortunate to be able to learn from their misfortunes and mistakes. We will forever be students of real-world gunfights because that's how we determine what works and what fails. We pride ourselves on being "Sometimes an instructor, always a student."

Entire volumes have been written comparing training on the range to performance on the street. For those new to the subject, let me illuminate just a few examples. The industry standard of firearms training 40 years ago was a complete joke by today's standards. The California Highway Patrol (CHP) is a good example. CHP officers were shooting .38's on the range and carrying .357's on the street. They were trained to dump the empty brass into their hand after a firing exercise and to place that brass in their pocket so as to keep the range spiffy. They were taught to reload their revolvers a single round at a time. They were taught almost nothing about the pump-action shotguns they were carrying in the cars. All of these deficiencies resulted in the deaths of four CHP officers one night in April of 1970 in Newhall, just outside of L.A. From the Newhall shooting emerged the current training standard of practicing with your carry ammunition, dumping empty brass to the ground, reloading revolvers six rounds at a time using a speed loader, and training with every weapon you might encounter. This all seems pretty basic today, but good men had to die to spark change.

In April of 1986, the FBI in Miami was hunting for a couple of murderous bank robbers who were leaving quite a bloody wake behind them. The FBI agents spotted the suspects driving in a Miami suburb. The agents rammed the suspect's vehicle which brought all the cars to a stop and now the action really began. Most of the FBI agents wore no body armor at all, even though they knew the bad guys were very fond of shooting people. The FBI agents were primarily carrying handguns in .38 or 9mm, even though they knew their adversaries would likely be shooting rifles and shotguns. Finally, the FBI largely got very poor hits on the bad guys. In the end, the two criminals expired at the scene, as did two FBI agents. Another five agents were seriously wounded. So, with reverence to the fallen FBI agents, what did we learn from all of this? The Miami FBI shooting resulted in better training on the use of cover and concealment, more widespread use of body armor, and the mandate to use long guns instead of handguns whenever possible. It also gave rise to the .40 S&W cartridge which is now a very common defensive handgun caliber, both in law enforcement and private hands. Yet, the most noteworthy training element to emanate from the Miami shooting is that of Combat Mindset. Some of the bad guys out there are not just sitting on the couch getting high and watching TV. Some of them have military training and keep their skills sharp with routine practice. These are serious enemies and such was the case in Miami. When you are confronted by a dedicated opponent, you need to be tougher. You need a Combat Mindset which is superior to your enemy's. One of the FBI agents had exactly that, and even though he was seriously wounded, he finished the fight.

In April of 1999, two disgruntled students at Columbine High School started shooting their fellow students inside the school. The first shots were fired at 11:19 a.m. The 911 calls went out immediately as gunfire and screaming filled the air. Every nearby agency responded and the officers gathered to talk about their options. Lengthy discussions ensued about jurisdictions, tactics, rescuing the wounded, determining good guys from bad, bomb threats, etc. More gunfire and screaming. More 911 calls. The shooting continued for 49 minutes, until 12:08 p.m. SWAT entered the building at 1:09 p.m. which was 110 minutes after the shooting started and 61 minutes after the shooting stopped. The only task remaining was to count the bodies; 13 students and teachers were dead. Add the two bad guys who committed suicide for a total of 15. Americans were outraged at the approach that law enforcement took at Columbine, even if it was in accordance to departmental policy. Waiting, studying, and setting up perimeters, is no way to stop the bad guys and save innocent lives. George Patton was correct in his estimation that a good plan executed now is better than a perfect plan executed later. And that is the exact offshoot of the Columbine mayhem. Most law enforcement agencies now have a firm "Active Shooter" policy which simply states go in and shoot the bad guy, as soon as possible, and worry about other things later. It seems so intuitive, doesn't it? But "Go shoot the shooters" was not departmental policy until after Columbine. The Active Shooter policy has saved numerous students and staff since 1999 and the Virginia Tech shooting in 2007 is an example. Yes, it was bad; but without the lessons learned from Columbine, it would have been far worse.

The above shootings are only three examples from a long list. But you get the point. At Front Sight, we attempt to integrate all these real-world examples into our curriculum. Clearly, we concentrate our efforts on you, the individual, and not team tactics, military units, and the like. Even so, there is benefit to be had, lessons to be learned, from each and every gunfight. Our goal at Front Sight is to make sure you receive that benefit.

In 1992 I had a lengthy conversation with a very notable figure in the firearms training world. He said flatly "There is nothing more to learn in the world of defensive shooting. The only thing left is dissemination. Spread the word and get people trained." I agree with the "get people trained" part of his statement. I completely disagree with the "nothing more to learn" part. That comment was made to me almost exactly 20 years ago. The advances made in terms of techniques, equipment, and tactics in the last 20 years are impressive. If we had simply declared ourselves victorious and stopped learning, we would have missed them all. You can stop learning if you want to, but the bad guys are a creative lot; they are sitting around right now dreaming up new ways to pull off their next stunt.

TINNITUS FOR A WEEK

Ask your shooting buddies if they have ever accidentally fired a shot. The answer is almost universally "Yes." These stories often involve the demise of a television, a light switch, or a car door. I have also heard of perforated windshields, headlights, fire extinguishers, air conditioners, wine bottles, couches, sliding glass doors, and family portraits. Over the last 25 years, I'll bet I've heard 500 such stories. The accidents involving only material items are embarrassing, and usually pretty funny. Yet sometimes, the story ends in tragedy.

Years ago we called the accidentally-fired shot an "Accidental Discharge." Seems logical. But on further review, there was really nothing accidental about it. The loud, unexpected "Bang!" was the result of negligence. The violator neglected one or more of the Four Universal Firearms Safety Rules. As such, for the last 20 years or so, the name has appropriately been "Negligent Discharge," or ND. I know you remember the four safety rules…obviously. But, just in case there is someone looking over your shoulder who might need a refresher, here they are:

1. Treat every weapon as if it were loaded.
2. Never let the muzzle cover anything you are not willing to destroy.
3. Keep your finger off the trigger until you are ready to shoot.
4. Be sure of your target, and what's in line with your target.

Okay, so how do you get an ND out of all that? Usually by ignoring Rules 1 and 3. You make the assumption that the gun is unloaded and start fiddling with the trigger. That combination guarantees tinnitus for a week.

Just for the record, I want to state clearly and emphatically, that the following story occurred before I received any training! So, it is with some degree of trepidation and embarrassment, that I tell you my ND story. I was a junior in high school and my mother had recently bought me a Colt Python .357 revolver. I loved that gun, especially its high-polished nickel finish! I had just changed the oil in my truck and was in the kitchen washing my hands. The phone in my bedroom rang so I shook the soapy water from my hands and dashed back to answer it. My buddy Jon was on the line and my Python was on the night stand. What better thing to do than mess with a loaded revolver, with wet soapy hands, while talking to my buddy on the phone? I was sitting on the bed and pointing the gun at the wall which separated my room from my brother's room. As commonly seen on TV, I was thumbing the hammer back and then pressing the trigger and easing the hammer forward by holding it back with my thumb…my wet, soapy thumb. After about 10 repetitions of this silliness, the hammer slipped from under my thumb. Jon hollered "What the hell was that?"

The bullet was a 158-grain Federal Hydra-Shok. It hit the wall at a slight upward angle about four feet above the floor. The room was filled with smoke and I couldn't hear a thing. I immediately set down both the gun and the phone. I actually checked my ears to see if they were bleeding. I wondered for a moment where the bullet went when it dawned on me that surely it went into my brother's room. Was he home? I had no idea. I instantly felt a wave of anxiety and adrenaline. I ran the 20 paces out of my room and into his, fully expecting to encounter a sucking chest wound. It took a second to determine that my brother wasn't there because the air was completely filled with a fine, white powder. I looked over at the wall and saw the gaping hole created by the .357 bullet. I was shocked that such a small bullet could make a fist-sized hole in the drywall. That's when I realized what the airborne white powder was.

I ran to the next bedroom in line to see just how far the bullet had gone. That next bedroom contained no damage; no indication of the chaos taking place just one room away. Back in my brother's room, I started hunting for the bullet. Following the path of the bullet was pretty easy based on the drywall damage. The bullet blasted through the first wall which obviously caused the gaping hole. Subsequently, it flew across the room at about chest height hitting the opposite wall. Instead of penetrating, the bullet carved a sizeable canyon in the drywall and was deflected almost straight up. It plowed into the ceiling, again tearing up the drywall but not penetrating. From the ceiling, it headed back toward my room; the original wall from which it entered. Again, another skid mark in the drywall, but no penetration. The bullet came to rest on the bed…beautifully mushroomed, just like it shows on the box.

So let's review. I launched a .357 bullet into my brother's room. It whirled around inside the room, tearing up absolutely everything. And it didn't kill my brother. When I realized just how lucky I was, I felt weak and had to sit down on the dust-covered bed.

That ND was a major event in my life and I remember it as if it happened yesterday. Not long after that, I got formal training and fully embraced the Universal Firearms Safety Rules. I have never again had to feel the shock and anxiety of a negligent discharge.

How Good is Good Enough?

I wonder, do <u>you</u> actually need formal firearms training? Many people live to a ripe old age and never even get into a fist fight, let alone a gunfight. They lived their whole life completely untrained and completely without skill. Yet, for them, unskilled was good enough. You and I understand the only reason they were "good enough" was dumb luck. Do you want to bet your life, and more importantly the lives of your loved ones, on dumb luck? At the other end of the spectrum, if your job entails serving high-risk warrants on the "other side of the tracks," you need lots of firearms training. Most of us live somewhere in between. You don't want to trust your life to luck but you don't want to train to some lofty "professional gunfighter" standard either. You understand the value of training but you want it to be correct and appropriate to your needs. That's what this chapter is all about.

The first thing you need to do is define what kind of training you need and how much. That's not easy. An unpleasant truth about gunfighting is that you have to be pretty darn good for your very first gunfight. You don't have the luxury of losing a gunfight or two as you get better and better. There is no "warm-up." There is no progression from little league to the minors to the majors. When it's for blood, you had better be in the majors the very first time that handgun leaves the holster.

And here's another problem. It's impossible to predict just how good you need to be to win any particular gunfight. That clearly depends on the bad guys you are facing. Many bad guys are complete idiots and just a modicum of skill and a firm attitude on your part will save the day. However, some bad guys are highly skilled and dedicated, and to win that fight you will have to be pretty sharp.

There are lots of entities which offer "firearms training." Examples include the local gun store, the local range, the NRA, family, friends, and professional training organizations. However, since gunfighting is not a trial-and-error type of activity, go to a professional organization for your training. Obviously, I recommend Front Sight, but I am also a realist. If you live on the other side of the country and your schedule or budget preclude you from making the trip to Front Sight, no problem. For the time being, get the best training you can at the local level. In fact, many of our students start at the local level to learn a little bit about the gun, shoot a few rounds, and get over their anxiety. Then they take the next step and come to Front Sight for professional training. There is nothing wrong with this two-step approach. Just don't kid yourself that a familiarization course held at the local range equates to proper training.

Defining the skills you will need on any particular day is impossible. I can however, describe for you a hypothetical gunfight, as it would be experienced from your perspective:

- You are using the Color Code of Mental Awareness and you see trouble brewing well in advance.
- You spot two or three suspicious guys who look intent on hurting you.
- You move to cover, or at least concealment, to get some protection.
- You deliver verbal commands which are crisp, clear, and rehearsed. These will hopefully dissuade your opponents, but at very least, help you later with criminal and civil liability.
- By now your heart is really racing and you rely on the Combat Mindset to stay focused.
- The distances are anywhere from arms reach to maybe 30 feet.
- The bad guys ignore your commands and make their move.
- You draw your handgun from a holster which is concealed under your shirt.

- You fire two rounds to the thoracic cavity of each adversary. To do that you again rely on the Combat Mindset to focus on the front sight, gently press the trigger, and completely ignore the bright flashes coming from their guns.
- It is all over in about 2½ seconds.
- You look around for more trouble because rats travel in packs.
- Your weapon is now half empty so you perform a Tactical Reload to bring it back up to full capacity.
- Now it's time to call 911 and get help. What you say and what you don't say is critical. It is so critical that it is rehearsed. Don't think for a second that you will be calm enough to deliver coherent information after having just survived a gunfight unless you have thought about it in advance.
- The cops arrive and they are as nervous as you are. If you do something silly now, you are at risk all over again for getting shot. This interaction is also rehearsed well in advance.

And here are a few variables which occur fairly often in the world of gunfighting:
- Your opponent has taken a loved one hostage. Now it is up to you to make a precision brain shot on the bad guy who is hiding partially behind your daughter.
- The bad guys are wearing body armor but you don't notice it. You get good hits but they don't work; your adversaries aren't impressed in the least. Now you are forced to use "Plan B." You had better have a Plan B!
- Your adversary turns out to be the guy standing right in front of you at the bank. He is so close to you that if you shoot from your usual stance, he will simply grab your weapon. You either need an alternate stance or more distance, or both.
- You ran your weapon out of ammunition and now it's time for an Emergency Reload.

- Somewhere along the line your weapon malfunctioned and you must clear it <u>right now</u>, before you get shot.
- The bad guy is inside your house and your family is screaming for your help. You called 911, of course, but the cops won't be there for 15 minutes. It's now up to you to move tactically and clear the house to help your family.
- It's too dark to reliably navigate through the house, or identify the threat, or see your sights. You must now add a flashlight into the equation to find and stop the bad guy.
- You are carrying a small child or maybe you are injured. Now you have to do all of the above with only one hand.

This is sounding more and more like professional training, isn't it?

BLUE ROOM BLUES

F<small>RONT</small> Sight has a large, modern, restroom facility centrally located on Range 4. The restroom facility is certainly nice, but it doesn't produce any funny stories. We have to look to the past for those.

As Front Sight was being developed, we did not yet have permanent restrooms and instead used portable toilets and hand wash stations. We placed the portable toilets adjacent to the classroom, ranges, and simulators. We routinely had 50 units or more in service at any given time. Our original toilets were blue in color which gave rise to a variety of nicknames such as "blue room" and "blue loo." I know; lame and childish. Remember, we are firearms instructors, not poets. We subsequently upgraded our toilets to a model that was desert tan in color. The nickname became "brown room," heaven forbid!

During my years in academia, I learned all about spontaneous combustion. I was always intrigued with spontaneous combustion because it seemed so unlikely. All you need are a few oily rags piled up in the wrong spot, and a healthy dose of patience. Back in the summer of 2003, we had a portable toilet staged near the gun cleaning area. After a day of cleaning guns, one of our guys filled a 5-gallon bucket with oily rags and set it on the ground adjacent to the blue room. The next day I arrived to an amorphous lump of black and blue plastic which stood only about a foot high. The soil around the plastic lump was stained dark blue. I asked one of our maintenance guys "What's this mess?" He asked right back "What do you think?" I studied the lump a bit harder because I'll be damned if I was going to be outwitted by one of the maintenance guys! I asked

"Is this the toilet?" "Was," said smartass. I felt cheated that I had missed the entire show. Naish was pissed that we had cooked a toilet. For a full month, the jokes about "hot pot" and "who was the last one in there?" were rampant.

The door handles on the blue rooms are color-coded to let you know if someone is inside. The color scheme is really simple, just like a stop light. Red means the door is physically locked and toilet is occupied; go find a different one. Green means come on in. And so I did. I know ladies often like to "hover" instead of sit. But this gal was standing on top of the toilet seat, I suppose to maximize her distance from the "splash zone." As we say in tactics "Distance is your friend!" She was squatting, doing her thing, which put her midsection at about the same level as my eyes. I have no idea where her pants were. This all played out in a split second, and that's one second of my life I would like to erase.

During a Q&A session I was conducting one afternoon, a student named Ernie raised his hand. He said he had a question about the portable toilets. "Would it be possible to remove the sharp edges from the front of the molded plastic toilet seat? When I sit down, those sharp edges cut my...well...my man parts." Holy shit; there are so many things wrong with that scene I don't even know where to begin. The most obvious question is "Why are your man parts coming into contact with ANYTHING in the blue room?"

As our student numbers grew, we needed to purchase additional portable toilets. Richard, one of our full-time Range Masters, suggested that we purchase the fancy units which actually flush. Apparently the solids are deposited onto a gently-sloping platform and are then flushed to the back and into the holding tank by means of a foot plunger. No more risk of the "blue splash!" Naish was not convinced but Richard showed him all the literature, and besides, they cost only a little bit extra. Naish begrudgingly agreed and we purchased a dozen of these units. With the very first "deposit" in these toilets, we discovered a slight problem. These toilets had to be on a perfectly level surface or the flush feature was useless. The deposit would sit right there, waiting to greet the next user. Naish was livid. He pulled Richard off of the range, gave him a wooden survey stake, and told him to go toilet-to-toilet all day long pushing turds down the hole! Richard was quickly on his cell phone calling the distributor to come swap out these goddamned fancy toilets for basic ones!

In the areas of highest student concentration, such as near the classroom, we would place a bunch of portable toilets side-by-side. This meant that the occupants of the adjacent toilets would be separated by two plastic walls, but they were still pretty close to each other. One of our female First Family members had a little problem with this arrangement. Apparently, proximity to others, or even the risk of proximity, stems her flow. Every time she took a course, she would politely demand that we move one toilet off by itself, maybe 30 feet or so, so she could have some privacy. No problem. We were happy to segregate a single potty away from the herd just for her. The maintenance guys took to calling this setup "Solitary Confinement." A clever lot they are.

On occasion, we would find some graffiti in the portable toilets. I never saw the old classics like "Here I sit cheeks a flexin' - giving birth to another Texan" or "For a good time call…" The Front Sight graffiti was fairly pedestrian. Here are a few examples:
- You're making a mess. Install a front sight on that thing!
- I love this place!
- If you aim at nothing, you will surely hit it.
- HEMI (this one appeared right after an instructor, now gone, bought a Dodge Charger!)
- Glock is good. Glock is great.
- I ♥ Naish

Naish is a popular guy, even in the blue rooms!

The portable toilets we had were pretty upscale in the world of porta-potties. They certainly weren't the putrid affairs we've all seen at the city park. Ours were relatively new and well appointed, if I do say so. They had a sink with flowing water, liquid soap, paper towels, and even a coat hook. We spent a ton of money having them serviced so they were generally quite clean. There is one place however, which could never be considered clean; down the hole, in the "splash zone."

(At this point in the story I am going to change Frank's name to "Hank" to protect his identity.) Here is the setting. We were running a variety of courses that weekend, including Advanced Tactical Handgun. We had a young man named Noble in that course. Noble needed to use the restroom and so chose the last unit in a row of three. Getting dressed after his biological effort, Noble dropped a Glock 22 handgun magazine down the hole. Noble thought little of it because he would simply grab another one of his dad's 100+ magazines. Upon leaving the blue room, Noble commented casually to ~~Frank~~ Hank about his magazine mishap. Noble thought no more of it and went back to

186

continue his training on the Tactics range. Hank wanted to locate that magazine and return it to its rightful owner, so he got busy. Hank didn't know which of the three toilets contained the magazine. No problem. Hank started searching the dark, watery abyss for Noble's magazine…using his bare hands! (It was okay though because he had his sleeves rolled up.) Hank squished his way through all the solids and determined that the magazine was not in Toilet #1. Nor was it in Toilet #2. Eureka! Hank found the submerged magazine in Toilet #3. Hank rinsed off the magazine and promptly walked over to the Tactics range to return it. Hank was surprised at the cool reception he got from Noble.

As Operations Manager I have enacted all sorts of policies. There is one policy I never thought would be necessary…KEEP YOUR HANDS OUT OF THE TOILET.

JUDGING A BOOK BY ITS COVER

WHEN I was a second-year graduate student, the university opened a "Career Center." I had no idea what it was but we were encouraged to make an appointment. As I later found out, the folks at the Career Center coach students on how to create a resume, prepare for job interviews, and successfully join the workforce. These days, "career prep" at most universities is a semester-long, three-credit course...and mandatory. Back then, it was a fairly novel idea.

I went into the Career Center at the appointed time with a draft resume in hand. I sat down across from a very homely, administrative type and I distinctly remember thinking "Those who can't do...teach. This lady looks completely unemployable and yet she is going to teach me how to launch my career?" And, with that not-so-open mind, we began dissecting my resume. Ten minutes into it, I realized, "Damn, she's good." Her word selection, sentence structure, and elaboration on just the right points amazed me. I left the Career Center hopeful that I may someday actually have a career! But at the same time, I knew that my new resume, while totally truthful, was a clear example of "accentuate the positive." I had the sneaking suspicion that if she could make me look good, she could make anyone look good.

It was with that lingering distrust of resumes that I would later evaluate hundreds of them at Front Sight. I have learned through my time in the "School of Hard Knocks" that resumes generally come in three categories:

1. <u>Crappy resumes from unqualified candidates.</u> This one is pretty self-explanatory. If the resume is lousy, the process stops right there. They get a thank-you note

instead of an interview.

2. <u>Excellent resumes from excellent candidates.</u> This, of course, is what I hope for. The resume is well constructed and accurately reflects the person's high level of skill. This is the person I want to interview, and in all likelihood, hire.

3. <u>Excellent resumes from unqualified candidates.</u> This is the "false positive." The resume looks really good and the person gets an interview. However, during the interview process, the wheels fall off. The resume grossly overstates the person's abilities. This person got help with their resume at the "Career Center." This person gets a handshake, but not a job.

As you can imagine, I have received untold numbers of resumes over the years. They come to me via every means imaginable. E-mail is the most common, but sometimes they arrive directly at my house by snail mail. I once received a resume that was sent by FedEx Priority Overnight <u>from England</u>. People also hand them to me face-to-face. I even received a "resume" which was hand written on a torn-open ammunition box, and tucked under the windshield wiper of my car:

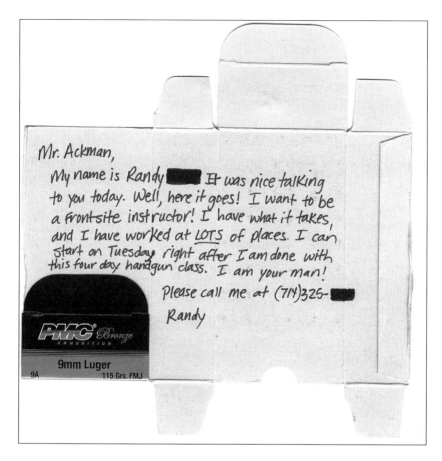

The "Ammo Box Resume." December 2006.

Whether the medium is an ammo box or the finest linen stationary, at least spell the name of the company correctly. If only I had a dollar for every resume I have received with Front Sight misspelled as Front Site, Frontsight, or Frontsite. Can you imagine sending a resume addressed to "Micrasoft," "Smithen Wesson," or "Catapillar"?

Perhaps I am overly conservative, but I think a resume should exude a clean, professional look. For example, the formatting should be simple, the font should be Times New Roman or maybe Arial, and the type size should be 11 or 12. It is difficult to take a resume seriously when it is written in 16-point, bold, italicized, Elephant font. Yes, Elephant! That's exactly what I received recently and it looked completely adolescent. Here is the opening paragraph of that cover letter:

March 3, 2012

Attn: Brad Ackman
Front Sight Firearms Training
Institute

Dear Brad,

It has come to my attention that there may be an employment opportunity within Front Sight for an individual with my interests and qualifications.

A couple of years ago, I received a resume the likes of which I had never seen before. This gentleman had obviously looked online for a resume template. He found one he liked and printed it. Then he wrote his resume onto that template, <u>literally</u>:

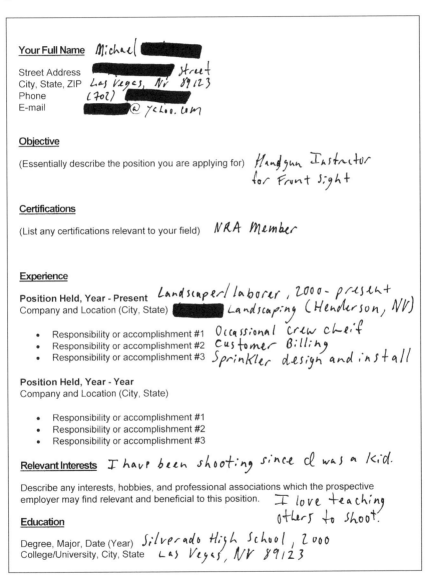

I received this "resume" back in the summer of 2010.

Years ago, a "proper" resume was a single page. That's it, period. Don't even think about a second page. That mindset has softened and seeing two or three page resumes these days is common. In October of 2010, I received an e-mail which had a resume attached as a PDF file. The first page was written in prose, not in resume form. So was the second page. So were all 27 pages! This thing was a novel, or at least a short story. Everything this guy ever did, every idea, was documented in his "resume." He even wrote about his newborn son who received an Apgar score of 8. No B.S.!

A resume is designed to be a glimpse of the person as a whole. If the resume is neat, well organized, exhibits proper spelling, and enjoys a logical flow of ideas, then that says a lot. So does the other end of the spectrum. Here is a particularly egregious "resume" which I received in January of 2012. I copied it directly out of an e-mail and I have left all the mistakes unchanged so you get the full flavor.

hey brad

well as soon as tax returns come ill be able to put a deposit down on a apt so ill be able to move out there and start full time. As soon as i know when i can move ull be the first to know, as far as the info goes i have studied phyc in high school, i hold a permit for ccw in mississippi, i have been a manager for almost all my jobs, the only one worth mentioning is 7-11. out of work now, but i was good at managing inventory like slurpee mix, candy, drinks, magazines, and such. I have studied econ. I am also in the process of learning the trade of home gunsmithing. The only other thing i can think of is my IQ was last tested at a 115. I do hope this helps you out and if you have any questions feel free to ask.

I know you think I fabricated the above resume as some sort of creative writing project. I assure you, the only change I made was deleting the sender's name!

I was presented with a resume back in 2003 from a gentleman named Joaquim. It was a very impressive resume; well-written and listed all sorts of accomplishments. Apparently Joaquim was a serious martial artist, an executive protection specialist, a defensive driving instructor, and a firearms instructor. In addition, he spoke six languages; English, Spanish, Catalan, Portuguese, Japanese, and Mandarin Chinese. "We'll just see about that," I thought and I hatched a plan. I was fortunate to have a variety of staff members who spoke other languages fluently. I called my guys and we set up a rolling interview. I called Joaquim first and conducted a phone interview in English. As soon as I hung up, John called Joaquim right back and conducted another interview in Spanish. Ten minutes later, Mike called and did the same thing in Portuguese. Then Bill in Japanese and Eddie in Mandarin Chinese. I had nobody on staff who spoke Catalan so I could only test five of the alleged six languages. When all the interviews were complete, we had a brief conference call. The result; Joaquim was the real deal. Not only did he speak the advertised languages, he spoke them fluently, with ease. I was impressed, and Joaquim was hired. And now I had someone on staff who was fluent in Catalan! After the Joaquim experience, I started to once again look at resumes with a faint glimmer of hope.

THURSDAYS

You know that heavy, dark feeling you have before you pay the monthly bills, or file your taxes, or study for final exams? For years, that's how I felt on the Thursday mornings before every Front Sight course. Thursday was setup day in preparation for the course starting on Friday. Thursdays meant a dozen tedious hours of labor and preparation. And when it was all done, there was precious little to show for it. Nobody had been trained. No money had been made. There was just fatigue. Yes, Thursdays was miserable, but it was still the most important day of the week.

Orchestrating large courses is a bit like painting your house. The key to success is in the preparation. Everyone knows you can't simply stir the paint, grab a roller, and get busy. First comes the patching, caulking, sanding, and masking. For every hour of actual painting, there was at least an hour of preparation.

Preparation is thankless. Nobody walks into a freshly painted room and says "Wow, you did a great job with the masking tape!" The same is true at Front Sight. Nobody arrives and says "Wow, look how all the trash cans are empty, all the water jugs are full, and all the rental guns are clean!" On the contrary, if you screw up the preparation...everyone notices. And everyone remembers.

These days, Front Sight runs courses nearly every day of the year. As such, preparation is a continuous process, handled by a sizeable, competent, maintenance crew running two shifts per day. That was not the case in the early days. When we first opened for business in April of 1996, we used a range called Global Security Complex located about 20 miles south of

Bakersfield, California. Our original setup crew was the instructional staff...in uniform...the morning of the course! What a misguided plan that was. An hour before the students arrived, we started hauling steel targets to the range, stapling paper targets onto the cardboard backers, filling water jugs, and setting out the proper number of chairs. There we were...six instructors, breathing hard and sweating, uniforms dirty, just as the first students were arriving. It was immediately evident that we needed to set up the day before the course.

I contacted a temporary labor company in Bakersfield called Continental Labor. I explained that I needed two guys who were not afraid to work to report to Global Security Complex on Thursday at noon. One little thing I forgot; they need to speak English. That first day with my helpers from Continental was a little rough! After that, I was able to reserve a couple of English-speaking regulars named Adam and Derrick.

As student enrollment grew, we needed more ranges and setup was commensurately more involved. I added a couple more laborers and started the day at 8:00 a.m. instead of noon. I would begin the day with a little staff meeting. Everyone got a check sheet, a pair of gloves, and a Red Bull. I wanted no excuses! My goal was to completely finish setting up by 4:00 p.m. That would give me time to get back to the hotel, shower, eat dinner, practice my lectures, and be sound asleep by 9:00. Sometimes that plan actually worked, sometimes not. On one particular Thursday afternoon in October of 1996, a swirling dust devil came ripping across the facility. This thing was just like the tornadoes I had seen on the plains of eastern Colorado, except a little smaller. The destruction was complete. Every range and simulator was stripped clean of targets and cardboard backers. Every chair was overturned, along with all the trash cans. It was 3:30 in the afternoon and we had to start the entire setup process again. We finished around 10:00 p.m. using the headlights of the truck. Man, I hate Thursdays.

The staff at Global Security Complex was a band of misfits masquerading as shooters and gunsmiths. They were truly ignorant and unpleasant people. They actually reprimanded and scolded our every move, even though Front Sight was their largest revenue stream, and some months their <u>only</u> revenue stream. On one particular Thursday morning in May of 1997, I pulled up to Global and the front gate was closed and locked. I assumed the Global staff had simply forgotten to open it. I called them on the phone but I got no answer. I honked my truck's horn several times hoping that would get a response. Nothing doing. The last option was to jump over the gate and knock on the front door, which I did. The miserable, filthy, beach-ball of a human named Clyde who functioned as a "gunsmith" swung the door open and started swearing. In the middle of his tirade, he actually bladed-off as if to prepare for a gunfight. My half of the conversation was along the lines of "Come on Clyde, surely you jest. You are mad at me for wanting to come in and set up the ranges? And now you want to get in a gunfight? You are what, 65? You weigh 400 pounds. And you are carrying a gun that YOU built and therefore likely won't even fire. I am 33 years old, healthy, and fast. This is ridiculous. Just open the goddamned gate." He eventually opened the gate and I put my crew to work. That evening on the way out, I noticed that Clyde had spray painted our road sign with the universal red circle and diagonal slash, indicating "No Front Sight." A little acetone and a rag put us back in action. Have I mentioned my disdain for Thursdays?

On the afternoon of Thursday, July 31, 1997, Naish received a FedEx envelope containing a letter of resignation from our Director of Curriculum and all of his "yes men." I'll refer to this guy as "Doc," simply using the acronym derived from <u>D</u>irector <u>O</u>f <u>C</u>urriculum. (How clever I am.) The resignation wasn't a complete surprise because we'd had some difficulties with these guys over the previous few months. In short, they honestly felt that Front Sight's success had been due to their participation, their mere presence on the range. They never considered Naish's efforts; his unwavering vision of the world's best shooting school, his business acumen, or his tireless marketing efforts. Nope, it was all about them. In the end, of course, their resignations were a blessing and we enjoyed huge growth immediately after the door slammed behind them. Even so, on the coming Saturday morning, little more than a day away, we had 102 students scheduled for a free submachine gun course. And now there were exactly two Front Sight staff members left; Naish Piazza and Brad Ackman. Great, on top of all our other Thursday duties, we now have to create staff!

We contacted Mike Waidelich and some of his Bakersfield PD cohorts. Mike had previously entertained working with us at Front Sight but was not at all interested in working alongside Doc. "Hey Mike, guess what..." Mike was able to round up the likes of Johnny Wilson, Jim Ramos, Don Kruger, Paul Trent, and Bill Bailey. I was able to round up uniforms and hats. The embroidered nametags would have to come later! Problem solved.

Staff ✔

As it turned out, staffing would not be the biggest problem we would face for this event. Seems Doc and the boys weren't satisfied with merely quitting at the last minute. They also had a multifaceted plan to sabotage our subgun event.

We were holding the event in Las Vegas at the Desert Sportsman range just west of town. Someone from Doc's camp called Desert Sportsman and warned them to avoid Front Sight like the plague. "Front Sight has no staff, no insurance, and no money." A couple of conference calls between us, the management at Desert Sportsman, and our insurance agent, and we were back on track.

Range ✔

Then another issue arose. We had ordered 50,000 rounds of ammunition for the event from J&G Guns in Prescott, Arizona. Doc's crew discovered that our ammo was coming from J&G so they called and laid on the B.S. "Don't ship the ammo, Front Sight has no money." Tough luck, the ammo was already delivered to Bob Oliver, one of our instructors in Las Vegas. Bob lived with his elderly mother who stayed home alone during the day when Bob was at work. Doc's guys actually had the gall to call Bob's mother, pose as "Brad Ackman," and say "We'll be right over to pick up the ammo." Bob's mom was pretty feeble, but she was sharp enough to see right through that crap. I have this vision of a little old lady, sitting on the front porch, rocking back and forth in her favorite chair, sipping lemonade, cradling a loaded shotgun across her lap, and waiting for Doc's boys to drive up! Alright, another problem solved.

Ammo ✓

What else could go wrong? About then I got a call from Harry Lu at Stembridge Arms who was providing all the guns. Doc's toddlers had called Stembridge in an effort to stop delivery of the guns. More conference calls. More reassurances.

Guns ✓

Okay, I think that's everything. About then my phone rang again. Seems Doc and the boys had resorted to <u>calling our students</u>. I have no idea how Doc got their phone numbers, but he certainly did. Doc's clan called every student on the list and filled their heads with "The event is cancelled," "Front Sight has folded-up," and "Come train with Doc instead." Naish and I went into high gear. I called every single one of the 102 students on the list. I assured them that we are alive, well, and looking forward to seeing them with an MP-5 in their hands on Saturday morning! A couple hours later, Naish called every single name on the list <u>again</u> and warmed their hearts even more.

Okay, let's review.
- Staff ✓
- Range ✓
- Ammo ✓
- Guns ✓
- Students ✓

This time I really do think that's everything. If Doc and his guys had only worked this hard while at Front Sight, things might have worked out differently.

Come Saturday morning, the weather was calm, overcast, and 85°. For August in Las Vegas, this was a luxury! I met our new staff for the very first time. "Hi, what's your name? Nice to meet you, you will be working with the Uzi's." "Hi, and you are? Great, nice to meet you, you will be on the MP-5 range."

Of the 102 people on the roster, 92 showed up. Naish discussed with the students the silliness of the previous few days and reassured everyone present that Front Sight is alive and well and here for the long haul. Then we headed to the range. We put on one hell of a show and the students had a great time. At the conclusion of the day, almost every single student shook our hands and thanked us for our perseverance. This was a huge show of support for Front Sight as an organization and Naish as an individual. This was the only time I have ever seen Naish Piazza show any emotion other than dogged determination. He is as tough as nails and has developed Kevlar skin from years of putting his name and reputation on the line to further Front Sight's mission. However, that particular day, the flood of student support he received brought him to tears.

This was a major turning point for Front Sight. It was clear now that people come to Front Sight for the training and the experience. They don't come to see any one individual. Front Sight is about the students, not the staff.

By Saturday night, I was wrung out. We had bested Doc's every attempt to stop our subgun event. We had recruited new staff and they did an excellent job. And, most importantly, our students were happy and supportive. Man, I could use some sleep.

Thursday April 16, 1998 was at the tail end of a very dramatic El Niño winter in California. The rain had been relentless in the valleys and the snow pack in the mountains set a new record. When spring arrived and all that snow started to melt, the flooding was horrendous. I knew that range setup at Global was going to be a bad deal so I came equipped with hip boots, shovels, and tow straps.

As it turned out, I couldn't even get to Global because the road was completely washed out in several places about a half mile from the front gate. The upstanding citizens who owned

Global knew well in advance of my arrival that the road was destroyed but thought it would be entertaining to watch us struggle. Struggle we did.

The road leading into Global Security Complex was completely washed out by El Niño flooding. April 1998.

A different, equally depressing, view of the road leading into Global Security Complex. April 1998.

I put on my hip boots, grabbed a backpack, and started walking. When I arrived at Global, I was shocked to see just how bad things were. The rifle range was completely submerged, the parking lot was flooded, the power was out, and the water was contaminated. (Hmm, all this damage couldn't have happened to a more deserving bunch.) I took a few photos and filled my backpack with small stuff. There was nothing else I could do. All of our supplies were being held hostage by raging flood waters and washed-out roads.

I called Naish to report the grim news. Most people would have caved-in hearing that news. Most people would have quit. Most people would have thrown up their hands and exclaimed "Nothing we can do…freak of nature…act of God…cancel the course." Not Naish. He understood the hurdles students must overcome to attend a course such as take vacation time away from work, take time away from family, and reserve airline flights, hotel rooms, and rental cars. No way a little flood, or even a huge one, was going to derail a Front Sight course.

Naish immediately started working on an alternate location for tomorrow's course. There was a range north of Bakersfield known as 5-Dogs Range and apparently the road in was passable. 5-Dogs it was. Naish got on the phone and called every student on the roster and let them know that Global was sunk, literally, and to meet us in the Home Depot parking lot tomorrow at 7:00 a.m.

All our students and staff met at the prescribed Home Depot and we caravanned to 5-Dogs Range. Pulling into the parking lot was the very first time I had ever seen this facility. Did they have some targets we could use? Did they have a classroom we could lecture in? How about toilets? Did they have a shoot house we could use as a simulator? This was last-minute setup at its finest and it definitely tested my organizational abilities. By now, the students were feeling like part of an adventure, and I recruited them to assist with range setup. In about an hour, we had moved enough crap off of the ranges so that we could actually use them. Someone found a bunch of generic B-27 targets and we hung them up. Additionally, we pushed all the random drums, tires, and other debris into something resembling a shoot house. We were completely out of luck for a classroom. However, the weather was gorgeous so we simply lectured outdoors. Man, did we get lucky on that score! At the end of four days, our students were very happy with the training and were excited to have played a role in Front Sight history. Handshakes all around.

Okay, so we dodged a bullet on that particular course. Now let the real work begin. By now, the flood waters had receded and it was time to rescue our supplies. On Thursday April 23, we started the mass exodus from Global Security Complex to our new home at 5-Dogs. I really hoped this was going to be a simple load-and-go operation. Of course, this was a Thursday, so that was not to be.

First, the road into Global was completely destroyed and would remain destroyed for months to come. To find an alternate way in, I drove all of the likely farm roads surrounding Global until I found a possible new approach. I located one miserable, mud-pit of a trail which spanned the two miles between the paved county road and Global. This trail followed the edge of a huge plowed field operated by the agricultural titan Grimmway Carrots. This trail was in terrible shape; two miles of mud, potholes, and ruts. I was not at all certain I could get a caravan of trucks across that trail, and out again, but it was our only hope.

Once I had identified a potential way in, I rented three trucks and a trailer from U-Haul and eight helpers from Continental. Getting all those vehicles over that pitiful, two-mile trail took more than an hour, but we did it. In our wake, we left the trail in worse shape than we found it, complete with numerous deep ruts. This was a serious concern because that trail was our only way out.

When we pulled into Global, the scene was shocking. The mud was 12 to 18 inches deep. Six inches of water still covered the entire facility. The wind was blowing so hard that whitecaps were actually forming in the parking lot. This was going to be another long Thursday.

We loaded everything we could into those U-Haul trucks. However, we ran out of space and had to leave some stuff behind including a freezer, a gun safe, and five big, steel, range tables. Additionally, we left a 40-foot storage container and the shade structures which we had erected the previous year. The owners of Global saw their only stable source of income departing and they threw a fit. They vowed "You will never set foot on this property again and we are keeping all your leftover shit!" As I told you, these people were real peaches.

Now it was time to drive away. Easier said than done. Getting the empty U-Haul trucks over Grimmway Carrot Trail was tough. Getting the fully-loaded trucks back over that same trail was nearly impossible. We spent several hours pushing, pulling, and digging our way back to the pavement. But again, we made it. It was well past dark now and we still had the 50-mile trek up to 5-Dogs. We must have looked like the Beverly Hillbillies; driving in a caravan, 45 miles per hour, and completely covered in mud. It took three days and six helpers to unload those trucks and make some sense of it all.

All that, and we still had to remove our last load of stuff from Global. Based on the attitudes and threats we received from the owners of Global, we clearly needed some legal assistance. We hired an attorney in Bakersfield who got to work on a temporary restraining order against Global. The judge granted the restraining order so we could again enter the property and collect our gear. However, the judge wouldn't allow us to remove our 40-foot storage container because he felt the truck necessary to move it might damage the already fragile roads. Great, another $3,000 down the drain.

On Thursday, yes Thursday, April 30, with restraining order in hand, we headed back to Global to get the last of our gear (minus the forbidden storage container). Also on the agenda was disassembly and removal of the shade structures which we had installed. To handle the shade structures, I requested the help of long-time Front Sight supporter Rick Kaufman and a rented boom truck. Once more over the Grimmway Carrot Trail. I anticipated problems with the Global folks and I really wanted to avoid bloodshed. Therefore, I solicited the assistance of the Kern County Sheriff's Office who made sure all guns stayed in the holster. As it turned out, there was plenty of bitching, but no gun play. When we pulled up to the range, some of our gear had been stolen! In the course of a week, the Global guys had stolen our moving target system and our beefy steel range tables. I had the Continental laborers start loading the U-Haul trucks while Rick and I began taking apart the shade structures. We placed all the wood, steel, and corrugated tin in a loose pile on top of a trailer for subsequent sorting and strapping. Just as we had all the pieces staged in a nice pile, a massive wind gust scattered it far and wide. Thankfully, nobody was cut in half by flying sheets of corrugated tin roofing. However, nearly every item in the pile was destroyed. We managed to salvage only three pieces of wood and one sheet of tin. What a waste.

That's it. We had the last of our stuff and we were forever done with Global Security Complex. I must admit, it was pure satisfaction watching Global disappear in the rear view mirror.

In January of 1999, we started running courses at our Nevada facility in addition to 5-Dogs in Bakersfield. The Nevada facility was still pretty spartan, so at first we only offered the free submachine gun events. After about six months, the Nevada facility was developed sufficiently to also support our standard courses (handgun, shotgun, and rifle). We ran courses at both locations for the duration of 1999. Starting with the new millennium, we were in Nevada only. However, during this year-long overlap period, Thursdays were really unpleasant. Back and forth between Nevada and California. One setup crew for Nevada, a different one for California. Some of our instructors worked in both locations, some only in Nevada, some only in California. I maintained one shopping list for Nevada, and another one for California. You get the idea. The whole world was excited to usher in 2000. I was simply satisfied to bid farewell to 1999!

Shortly after New Year's Day of 2000, we departed from 5-Dogs for the final time with our metaphorical sights set strictly on Nevada. Dave Olds and the crew at 5-Dogs were complete gentlemen and helpful right to the very end. Compared to the ragtag bunch at Global, dealing with 5-Dogs was like winning the lottery and Christmas morning, all rolled into one.

By about February of 2000, we were moving full speed ahead at our Nevada facility. The dome-shaped white tent, (complete with Astroturf for carpeting!) was installed and serving as our classroom. We finally had all of our equipment and supplies in one location, instead of split between two states. We had plenty of instructors and ample maintenance staff. We even had several guys living on-site serving as security to keep everything safe and sound. Things were consistent, predictable, and much more pleasant. Finally, I no longer needed to be on-site for Thursday setup. Be careful what you ask for. My Thursday workload simply shifted from true manual labor to administrative functions. And there were lots of them.

I soon became the lightning rod for people's problems, questions, and complaints on Thursdays. Everybody needed something the day before the course started. I actually counted my incoming phone calls on a given Thursday...84. The exactness of this number comes from the caller ID feature. Add to this my outgoing calls and the number was well over 100. That number would surely be scoffed at by some telemarketer in Mumbai, but to me it meant real work. Over the course of a 12-hour day, 100 calls meant the phone was up to my ear with a new call about once every seven minutes or so. Everyone had a question and nearly everyone had a problem. If I could answer the question immediately, I was quite happy. "Yes" or "No" followed quickly with "Goodbye." On the other hand, if I had to root around for an answer in the computer or one of my many file cabinets, I was less happy. If I had to listen to someone's tale of woe, or round up several people for a three-way call, I got downright surly. As much as possible, I would postpone the non-critical calls until the next Tuesday, following the four-day course.

The busiest, most hectic days of my life were Thursdays at Front Sight from 1996 through about 2001. Thursdays in the early years within Front Sight Operations were not for the faint of heart.

I've only landed in the Emergency Room twice in my life; both times on a Thursday. I've only been in one serious car accident…again on a Thursday. I'm not superstitious, really I'm not. But maybe we can drop Thursdays and switch to a six-day week!

DULL MINDS AND SHARP OBJECTS

Most of us at Front Sight are gun guys, not knife guys. I for one am wholly untrained in knives and thus default to the experts on the martial arts staff. However, being a red-blooded American male, I still like messing with knives! Untrained but enthusiastic. Surely, that must be a bad combination.

I had just bought a Cold Steel Super Mega Kahuna from our Pro Shop. This thing was huge; truly a short sword that folds in half. It came complete with a toothy serrated edge that was just looking for soft flesh to victimize. I know, I know. I have heard all the jokes. "You know what they say about the man who carries such a big knife?"

That very evening I was driving home from Front Sight and I called the Pro Shop from my cell phone. Anna, the lady who just sold me the knife, answered the phone. She heard the telltale "click-click" of the knife opening and closing. She warned me "You aren't playing with that knife are you?" "No, hell no," I said. As soon as we hung up, I folded that behemoth blade right down on top of my trigger finger. Great, now for the next few weeks, I'm not even a proper firearms instructor! I now realize that this incident must have been some sort of IQ test. Give a guy a Chevy Suburban, a cell phone, and huge honkin' knife. Whatever happens next is a pretty good indicator of his overall intelligence. Damn it, I want a do-over. I know I can do better!

I am not alone in this stupidity (and even if I were, I would fabricate a story to help diffuse my embarrassment.) We had a rifle instructor named Don who was quite accomplished with firearms, but not knives. He too, went out and purchased a sizeable knife. In his case, it was an eight-inch, double-edged, fixed-blade affair. Along with the knife he purchased a DVD on knife fighting. I forget the title, something like "Never-Before-Seen Knife Fighting Techniques of the Super Secret Black Ops Navy SEALs." Don started the DVD and took the knife out of its sheath, thereby removing the last bastion of safety. He started "shadow boxing" in front of the mirror, trying out some of the "classified" techniques he had just seen on the DVD. The next technique on the agenda was transitioning to a "reverse grip." This involved rotating the knife in the hand, point to the rear, and bringing the hand back alongside the hip. Well, he got the "rotate" part right, but he totally screwed up the "alongside" part. Don plunged the knife directly into the front of his hip, neatly slicing the femoral artery. He looked down in disbelief more than pain. Then, he pulled the knife out. Blood shot like a fire hose all over the mirror, just like you see on CSI. Thankfully, his wife was home and she had some medical training. Honey...HONEY!!!

Jeff Cooper was above all this silliness. He simply carried a little Swiss Army knife, safely folded up, deep in his pocket. It only came out when it was time to open a bottle of wine or tighten a screw.

"Get this thing away from me!" It takes a big man (with a bandage) to admit when he's made a mistake.

MY NORELCO SHAVER

During our long run of free submachine gun courses back in 2000, we got a call from a guy who was interested in submachine gun training. However, he didn't want the pedestrian, free version for the common man. No, he wanted <u>private</u> submachine training. No problem, we can certainly do that, and we told him the price. The caller identified himself as Gerald Braun, heir to the Braun empire of electric appliances. Gerald flatly said something along the lines of "Money is not an issue. In fact, if I like what I see, perhaps I'll invest in your little project." When it came time to actually commit to a schedule, Gerald decided to go with the free version of the course after all, which immediately cast a dark shadow of doubt over his story.

The day of his free subgun course, Gerald drove up in a Mercedes AMG coupe; jet black and pristine. Maybe this guy was the real deal after all. The day went just like so many before, smooth and uneventful. Gerald never mentioned anything about investing, taking another course, purchasing a membership, nothing. He simply thanked us and waved goodbye.

A few months later, I was driving home from a four-day course. Since I routinely transported a bunch of school weapons, I often carried an M-16 up front, just to keep me company. As I pulled into the cul-de-sac, I saw my wife standing at the end of the driveway, talking to a couple of guys. As I got a little closer, it was evident by my wife's body language that she wasn't happy. I looked over at the two guys. Hmm, that one there looks familiar. And then I saw the $150,000 black Mercedes. Ah, that's Gerald Braun. Who is this other guy standing next to him? And why are they facing my wife in a bladed stance, wearing untucked Hawaiian shirts? Shit, this doesn't look good.

I pulled my Suburban right into the middle of this little party. Conveniently, my wife was on the driver's side of my vehicle and the opposing team was on the passenger's side. I quickly stepped out and said in a friendly voice "Hi Gerald." I had the M-16 in hand but kept it out of sight next to the vehicle. I was trying the classic approach of "Speak softly and carry a big stick." God, I hope this works. If not, I can just see tomorrow's headline: "Rogue Firearms Instructor Guns-Down Electronics Billionaire in Las Vegas Suburb."

Gerald let loose with his complaint. "Your wife has been prank-calling me and I want it to stop!" I said "Surely you are kidding." He switched approaches and asked "Do you have any kids?" I replied "What possible difference could that make?" He shouted "Maybe it was your kid!" I asked Gerald "What makes you think anyone in my family has been calling you?" He launched into an agitated discussion which involved comments like "You have my phone number in your Front Sight files...calling my house at 3:00 a.m. and hanging up...my security team has investigated..." I assured Gerald that none of this applied to me. I concluded with "Thanks for stopping by, but now it's time to go." The two Hawaiian shirts looked at each other and slowly backed up to the Mercedes.

I filed a report with Las Vegas Metro PD the next day and hoped that I would never see or hear from Gerald Braun again. I wanted Braun out of my life forever.

Be careful what you wish for. My wife promptly trashed our Braun coffeemaker, Braun blender, and even my Braun shaver. She said, "I hope you can get along with Norelco."

KEVLAR ROAD SIGNS

I shot a highway sign once. And I still feel like an idiot. I was 15 years old and driving through Utah, heading home after flyfishing on the Green River. Still too young to drive, I was in my buddy's car and I was riding shotgun...or should I say "handgun." As we drove all those miles, I noticed that every single road sign had been shot. The large green highway signs had been shot dozens of times. I thought there must be something more to shooting road signs than meets the eye. If so many people were shooting so many signs, maybe I should try it; classic "herd" mentality. I wadded-up some paper towel to create make-shift ear plugs and I hauled my 1911 out of my fishing backpack. I poked my gun out the window and waited for the next sign. I think we just found the longest stretch of highway in Utah without a single road sign. Okay, there's one! It was a good-sized green sign depicting an exit and a right-hand arrow. It was mounted on a couple of galvanized steel posts relatively near the ground and the background was completely clear. I pointed at the sign and fired. I expected the classic "Bang-Ding" that I was used to on the range. "Bang" of the gun and "Ding" of the bullet hitting a steel target. Of course, highway signs aren't constructed of armor plate steel, but rather aluminum. Thus, when you shoot a highway sign, like a complete loser, the sound is more "Bang-Thud." And the bullet sails through the aluminum as if it weren't even there.

Immediately I felt like a fool. I had just perforated a highway sign and it wasn't even a difficult shot! I must be missing something. Probably the missing element was alcohol. Maybe hitting that huge green sign was tougher after a 12-pack! Thank goodness I will never know. And thank goodness nobody saw me or I'd get to explain my "just had to try it" logic to the Utah Highway Patrol. I obviously never shot a road sign again but there are lots of people out there who do.

We spent about $2 million on Front Sight Road which should actually be called "Front Sight Driveway." As such, we have a significant amount of pride in that four-mile stretch of asphalt. Front Sight Road is decorated with all kinds of signs; Speed Limit 45 MPH, Clark County, Nye County, Flash Flood Area, and a Stop at each end. There are 23 signs in all, and every single one has been shot. The "O's" in "Front" or "County" or "Flood" were the first to fall victim to bullet holes. Then came the shapes of crosses or T's because they too, make a nice aim point.

At least this guy managed two respectable "hand-span" sized groups.

This knucklehead clearly has a "Mashing" problem. He needs to come to Front Sight and learn proper trigger control. (In all likelihood, he wouldn't pass the background check!)

I dream of all sorts of wicked retribution for those who shoot our signs. Clearly, the best option would be a sign that simply shoots back! Next might be some sort of tire spike system which activates at the sound of gunfire. With four flat tires, the violators would be stuck and we could drive out to them and say "Hi." Hell, maybe we should simply invest in Kevlar road signs. Imagine that conversation. "Hi Naish, it's Brad. Listen, I know we just spent $2 million on the road but I'd like to spend another $750,000 on bullet-proof road signs. What do you think? Hello? Naish?"

SPRAY PAINT AND SNAKE OIL

HAVE you ever been to the SHOT Show? It is properly known at the Shooting Hunting Outdoor Trade (SHOT) Show. The name is wrong. It should be "Reinvent the Wheel Show." Most vendors there are trying to make a buck by modifying an existing product and then using adjectives like:

- Tactical
- Special Operations
- SWAT
- Urban Warfare
- Military Tested
- Rapid Deployment
- Heavy Duty
- Warrior Strength

Slings are a prime example. Rifle and shotgun slings are merely straps which allow you to put the gun over your shoulder so you have both hands free for other things. That's it. Granddad knew that. Hell, great-granddad knew that. But great-granddad was ignorant. He simply didn't know that he <u>needed</u> a sling which featured desert camo, black plastic D-rings imported from Italy, Velcro here and there, cute little straps which go around the buttstock and forend, little compartments to hold tools or ammunition, and bungee cords for extra comfort and sponginess. I am surprised great-granddad made it through the war or put venison on the table without all those features.

Gun coatings are another example of "reinvent the wheel." All the basic metal coatings have existed for decades, or even centuries. Bluing, Parkerizing, powder coating, anodizing, electroless nickel, and hard chrome have been protecting guns forever. That leaves the relatively new category of spray-on finishes. Such finishes are essentially spray paint. Those who are marketing spray-on coatings would vehemently disagree. They advertise their products with:

- Bonds to the metal
- Penetrates into the pores
- Thermo-set resin
- Multi-part epoxy
- Infused with porcelain
- Patented formula contains Teflon
- Reduces friction and wear
- Reduces glare
- Available in Desert Tan, Coyote Brown, and Iraqi Insurgent Red
- Available with special templates to create your own camouflage patterns including Mossy Oak, Realtree, Woodland, Urban, *Shadow* Urban, *Night Shadow* Urban, and *Subdued Night Shadow* Urban

Give me a break! What we are talking about here is basically Krylon spray paint!

There are numerous other categories of "reinvent the wheel." However, I will denigrate just one more: gun cleaners and oils. Since we evolved past "corrosive" powders decades ago, gun cleaning is pretty easy. The idea is to remove the carbon, lead, and copper. Then, a little lube allows things to run smoothly and protects the gun from the elements. The arena of cleaners and lubricants is rife with advertising silliness:

- Citrus based
- Soy based
- Organic
- Biodegradable
- Non-Toxic
- Food Grade
- Edible
- Moisture wicking

- Next generation
- For Law Enforcement and Military weapons only
- Lubricates from -100 to +550°F
- One application bonds to the molecules of the metal and lasts the life of the gun
- Prevents heat buildup
- Protects against hydrogen sulfide

What a joke. Now really, how could a thin film of oil "prevent heat build up" in a barrel where the burning powder reaches 3,000° F? Similarly, I never knew we needed to protect our guns from hydrogen sulfide. I know about hydrogen sulfide in the oilfields, but I couldn't think of any other common sources so I did a little research. The most common sources of hydrogen sulfide appear to be volcanoes, sulfur hot springs, pulp and paper mills, and swine manure. I can just see it now. "Gentlemen, this is getting serious. Before you dive headlong into the pig shit with your 1911 on, wipe it down with Snake Oil 2000!" Additionally, someday we may have to escape the post-Apocalyptic zombies by heading to the moon, or maybe even Mars. But before blastoff, wipe your gun down with Snake Oil 2000 because it offers protection even at those extreme temperatures. Also, I really hope I am never in the situation where I need to earn a paycheck by describing gun lubricant as "edible."

I know my opinions will be judged by many as arcane, out-of-touch, and simply fuddy-duddy. Understand, I am not stuck in the past. I relish all the advancements in the firearms industry over the years. Such advances include stainless steel, synthetic rifle and shotgun stocks, illuminated reticles, polymer handgun frames, Kydex holsters, and tritium night sights. Of course, there are others as well. But just because someone adds a Velcro tab, or blends two colors of spray paint into one, or puts a picture of an M-16 on a bottle of soybean oil, don't tell me that the world is now a better place.

Uzi's, Floozies, and the Ackman Challenge

"Gun nuts building a gated resort community in the Nevada desert!" "Crazy Chiropractor takes over Sin City with an Uzi!" Tag lines like these were all over the nightly news in Nevada, California, and across the nation. The media loved Front Sight's free, one-day, promotional submachine gun course because it had something for everyone:

- Fully-automatic submachine guns
- Controversy
- Attractive ladies
- A huge firearms "compound" in the desert
- Sin City
- A mixed bag of people and personalities from all across the country

Those one-day submachine gun courses were a hoot. And they produced some of the most colorful stories in Front Sight history.

As Naish was getting his firearms training in the late-'80's and early-'90's, he really wanted to shoot some fully-automatic weapons. He approached all the likely venues but received nothing but snubs. "Full-auto is only for the military and law enforcement," was the typical refrain. That was complete rubbish and Naish knew it. These outfits just didn't want to bother with the civilian market because they estimated its size to be inconsequential. What a gross miscalculation that proved to be. As soon as he was able, Naish put together the largest, grandest opportunity for private citizens to shoot submachine guns…for free! Ah, success really is the sweetest revenge!

With determination on his face, Naish Piazza rises, victorious, from the "Primordial Uzi." May 2002.

We ran our very first submachine gun course in January of 1997. It was a one-day event and the participants were ecstatic. We did it again six months later and got the same result. We held two more courses in 1998. By early-1999 it was clear that we had created something special and we switched to running them <u>four days per week</u>. That break-neck pace continued for almost three years!

Front Sight provided everything at the course free of charge. The day started at 7:00 a.m. with breakfast and ended at 3:30 p.m. with lunch. The hours in between were packed with legitimate, professional training on fully-automatic submachine guns. Of course, we also provided the ammunition free of charge, and each participant used roughly 300-350 rounds.

The "free" submachine gun course was free for the participants but was quite expensive for Front Sight. When you consider the instructional staff, guns and magazines, ammunition, weapons maintenance and cleaning, food, and advertising, each participant cost us roughly $200. Some days we had 50 participants, some days we had 300. These events were huge…and hugely expensive! What Front Sight received in return was priceless international exposure from venues like Good Morning America and Fox News. Additionally, we gave each participant the opportunity to purchase courses and memberships, and many took advantage of the offer. Front Sight was quickly becoming a household name.

We saw absolutely all walks of life in the subgun courses. Much like a bell curve, those folks in the middle did not stand out. But those on the fringes, I will never forget.

We saw a fair number of "free-loaders" who had no intention of doing anything with us besides eat free food and shoot free ammo. Sometimes it seemed like every derelict capable of holding up a thumb to hitchhike a ride was at Front Sight to shoot an Uzi.

We assumed that people would take the free subgun course only once. We should have known better. Remember when you were a kid doing the "trick-or-treat" circuit through your neighborhood on Halloween? When you found the house offering king-size Snickers instead of crappy little Tootsie Rolls or Hershey's Kisses, what did you do? Were you simply thankful that someone finally appreciated the size of your sweet tooth or did you change your costume a little bit and go back five more times? It seems those greedy little kids never actually grow up! They just find other venues to exploit.

We had a gentleman in his late-40's who took the subgun course in April of 2001. The weather that particular weekend was unseasonably warm so this guy wore a tank top which fully displayed his intricate tattoo. The tattoo was of a zipper which went up one arm, across the top of his shoulders, and down the other arm. He looked a bit like a cadaver which somehow came back to life. He also had long hair which he wore in a thick braid down the center of his back. A couple of weeks later, the weather was cool and windy and we had a guy in the class who wore his hair in a long braid. He looked vaguely familiar but I didn't recognize him because the zipper tattoo was hidden under a jacket. In mid-May, the weather was warm again and "Zipper Man" was back. This time I put it all together. In the span of a month, this guy had been to Front Sight three times, getting his fill of free food and submachine guns! I had a friendly chat with Zipper Man and encouraged him to come back and take the free subgun course again…only if he planned to purchase a membership!

At the end of each day, we asked the participants to complete a questionnaire and give us their feedback. One of the questions on the form asked how Front Sight could improve the free subgun course. One guy actually wrote that we should change up the lunch menu because pizza was getting old. Additionally, he wrote that we should offer a variety of guns to shoot besides just Uzi's, like maybe MP-5's and M-16s!

At the other end of the bell curve were the high-society, high-finance, and dot-com guys. Particularly in early-2000, the stock market was up, the dot-com guys were all billionaires, and everyone was happy. In January every year, the huge Consumer Electronics Show came to Las Vegas and brought with it lots of high-rollers, some of whom wanted to shoot a submachine gun. In a single day in January of 2000, we had an impressive array of expensive cars in our parking lot including a cream-colored Bentley, a pristine 1960's Jaguar, a jet-black Porsche 911 Carrera, a Maserati of some kind, and two stretch limos. One of the owners was still wearing his pin stripe suit, made of the finest wool/silk blend. He also wore a pair of fancy Italian goat skin shoes…with little tassels. At the end of the day, he seemed to take pride in how dusty his $1,000 shoes were, as if flaunting a disposable wardrobe! Yes, all are welcome at Front Sight.

Speaking of clothing, we saw the strangest getups you could imagine. You would expect a pair of jeans, hiking boots or running shoes, and a T-shirt when it's warm or a jacket when it's cold. By and large, that's what we saw. However, some people just have to be different. We had one lady show up with no shoes…of any kind. It's not like she forgot them at the hotel; she purposefully came out to Front Sight to shoot submachine guns in her bare feet.

Jeans are pretty handy because they have pockets to hold your car keys, a spare Uzi magazine, and a handful of ammo. But what about tiny little short-shorts or skin-tight, hip-hugging Yoga pants? What now? Well, we had to figure it out. Frequently in May and June when the weather was sunny and hot, we saw groups of ladies in their 20's and 30's who were clad in tiny little pants and scoop-neck, crop-top T-shirts. The midriffs were always bare and tramp-stamp tattoos were everywhere. There were three significant problems with this attire:

1. Yoga pants afford no storage for an Uzi magazine. One young lady tried to tuck the magazine under the waistband of her red lace thong which was peeking out of the top of her pants. That didn't work.
2. A scoop-neck T-shirt, coupled with a surgically augmented chest, forms the perfect funnel to catch flying brass.
3. In light of items 1 and 2 above, keeping the staff focused on submachine guns was damned difficult!

These ladies frequently arrived in groups of 5-10, perhaps to make the biggest splash possible. Sometimes we looked like an episode of "Girls Gone Wild" or "Maximum Wobble"…and that was before we started shooting! Even though the days were hot, I never had any trouble finding staff willing to work these subgun events. Pat, one of our Range Masters, quickly took to calling these situations "Uzi's and Floozies."

As Front Sight's free subgun course reached an international audience, we saw more and more people who couldn't even spell "Uzi," at least not in English. When it came to putting an Uzi in the hands of someone you couldn't talk to, a picture was worth a thousand words. Even better, a personal mime was worth a million words! We simply acted out, in very explicit detail, every move the shooter was to make. Marcel Marceau would have been proud.

We ran the free subgun courses four days a week, seemingly forever. They were fun as hell for the students but they became pretty routine for the staff. We needed to spice it up a bit to break the monotony. One of our Range Masters was somewhat of a semi-pro pyrotechnician. He was infatuated with anything that went "boom." He purchased some novelty exploding targets which were about the size of a Reese's peanut butter cup. The idea was to shoot the center of the target and it exploded in fairly dramatic fashion. These exploding targets had double-stick tape on the back so you could adhere them to a backstop.

One of the demonstrations during the subgun course was called "Failure to Stop." The idea here is you shot the bad guy a couple of times in the chest; the shots had no effect and the bad guy is still fighting, so you transition to a head shot. For this demonstration, we placed one of these exploders behind the head portion of the target. Nobody could see the exploder on the back side of the target so when that exploding target did its thing, the "Wow!" effect was huge. Yet, if a single exploder is good...I'll bet two is even better. Thanks to the double-stick tape, we were able to put a couple of them together, much like a pair of Lego's. Pretty soon we had 4-5 exploders behind the head for this demonstration.

One May afternoon in 2001, we threw caution to the wind and stuck eight of the exploders onto the back side of the head. From the front of the target, everything looked normal. The back of the target however, looked like Pinocchio! We gathered the students around for the big demonstration. The staff was absolutely giddy with anticipation! When I called for the head shot, Ron was so excited that he missed the exploders, hitting the target low in the chin. I called "Head!" again, and this time Ron hit. The entire target vanished in a white cloud of smoke and debris. The wood target frame sheared completely in half. The corrugated plastic target backer rained down in a million pieces the size of postage stamps. The paper target was completely vaporized. The crown jewel however, was the handful of drywall screws used to build the wood target frames. Seems we forgot all about those. These two-inch spears flew violently in all directions. Ron, the shooter, got one in the hat. I got one in the forearm. Nothing serious, just enough to drive home the point that we had crossed the line between adult and juvenile. That spelled the end of the exploding targets.

The final range exercise for the Uzi students was shooting the tightest group possible on full-auto, from five yards, with an entire 30-round magazine. In fact, the students did it twice and then took home their best target. Some of the students shot impressive, fist-sized groups. These were generally the guys who shot full-auto weapons on a regular basis or the big brutes who could hold the gun absolutely rock solid for 30 rounds and three seconds.

At 3:30 every day, Domino's delivered dozens of pizzas to feed the students and the staff alike. At that point, the students were dismissed from the range and went to the classroom to eat. Once the students were safely in Naish's care in the classroom, the staff was free to relax a little bit. For a little excitement, the staff had a variation on the "tightest group" theme described above. That variation was money. Yes, yes, we resorted to betting on who could shoot the tightest group on full-auto. The entry fee was $10 and winner takes all. We got pretty good with the Uzi's and it became difficult to determine the winner from a bunch of groups all the size of lemons. We had to back up to 10 yards just to discern who had the best group, and thus who walked away with the cash.

Once we had crowned the winner of the "tightest group," we sat down in the shade and ate lukewarm pepperoni pizza. From this casual scene, "The Ackman Challenge" was born. The Ackman Challenge was merely a light-hearted shooting competition among the staff, and it was pretty simple. Here were the rules:

- Gather some chairs around the pizza table and have a seat
- Prop your aching feet up on table
- Hold a slice of pizza in your support hand
- Hold your pistol in your firing hand
- Shoot five head shots from 25 yards
- The shooter with the best group wins and was exempt from hanging targets for the entire next day

It didn't happen often, but it was a good day when I emerged victorious with cash from the "tightest group" and bragging rights from "The Ackman Challenge."

Over the months, we ate dozens of Domino's pepperoni pizzas and I desperately needed a change. So, one fine day, I ordered pepperoni for the staff and vegetarian for me. When the pizzas arrived, they were all pepperoni. Damn it. In disgust, I picked off a slice of pepperoni and sailed it through the air like a greasy little Frisbee. It hit a target, and it stuck! Hmm, I wonder if I could hit that slice of pepperoni with my handgun from the 25 yard line. And that was the genesis of "The Ackman Challenge II, Perforate the Pepperoni." At first we actually stapled the slices of pepperoni to the paper targets. However, we soon learned that staples were unnecessary. The grease adorning a Domino's pizza was a cross between Elmer's Glue and earwax. It always held that little slice of pepperoni in place just fine. I am sure there is a moral to this story but I'm not sure what it is. Ask your cardiologist, maybe he knows.

In June of 2002, we bid farewell to the free subgun courses. We all got some well-deserved rest and even lost a few pounds.

WHAT'S IT LIKE?

I'VE been asked a hundred times what it's like working with some of the biggest names in firearms training. I can say this: the firearms training world consists of a diverse cast of characters. Some of them I have associated with continuously since the 1980's and they are my lifelong friends. Others, I associated with for only a few years and I was happy to leave them in the dust. I don't pretend to have a complete or accurate picture of all the big-name people in the firearms training world. That ignorance however, doesn't prevent me from having an opinion! I'll limit the scope of this chapter to the two biggest names in firearms training.

What's it like working with Naish Piazza?

First of all, I have never met anyone who works harder than Naish Piazza. Period. He is absolutely driven. He gets up early, he stays up late, and he works diligently every hour in between. As an example, when we were conducting courses in Bakersfield, Naish and I would share a room at the Holiday Inn Express. I would get to the room just after dinner, lay out my uniform, practice my lectures, and go to sleep. Conversely, Naish would work all day at his office, drive about five hours to Bakersfield, and arrive at the room around midnight or so. By then, I had been asleep for a few hours. That made no difference to Naish. Upon arrival at the room, he wanted to discuss the marketing and curriculum ideas he had while driving. I distinctly remember one such midnight conversation. It took place on the night when daylight savings mandates we move the clock ahead one hour. After a thorough debriefing, Naish asked me "So, what do you think?" I mumbled "I wish we had gained an hour tonight instead of lost an hour." He got the idea and turned out the light.

Naish is very intelligent. He has a high IQ, is well educated, and well spoken. For the first several years at Front Sight, he knew every single student by name and by voice. When a student would call the corporate office, Naish was routinely the one who answered the phone. If the student ever called again, Naish would immediately recognize the voice and promptly ask "Hi Jim, how are Judy and the kids doing?" Even if Naish never spoke to the student, he still knew them by their application. When Naish and the student crossed paths during a course, Naish would say something like "Sure, I know who you are. You live on Magnolia Street in San Diego." It was uncanny; a bit like a magic trick on the Las Vegas Strip.

Being "well spoken" is a double-edged sword, however. Ah, Naish does enjoy the spotlight! Be sure to set aside a few hours, and bring not one Red Bull but two, if you are going to join a Front Sight staff meeting or conference call.

Naish has real entrepreneurial vision and he thinks on massive scales. A prime example of that was in January of 1997 when several of us visited the naked Nevada desert which would someday become Front Sight. We stood in the early-morning sunshine on a small hill and looked around. Everyone there saw something different. Some saw sagebrush at their feet and pretty mountains in the distance. I could easily envision our facility right over there. Then I started planning. "Ideally, the road should run right through here, the power should come in overhead to about this point and then switch to underground, and the ranges should face north given the sunlight and prevailing southerly winds." Naish saw the Front Sight mission statement: thousands upon thousands of mainstream Americans coming to us to get the training they need, and opinion leaders from all over the world descending on Front Sight to join us in the fight to improve the image of gun ownership. That's what I mean by "vision."

Brad Ackman and Naish Piazza admiring the Nevada desert which would eventually become Front Sight Firearms Training Institute. January 1997.

Naish thinks right through barriers as if they don't exist. Of course, those barriers do exist and Naish knows it. He pays guys like me to overcome them. Naish is extremely aggressive when it comes to marketing. He is not one to sit around and ponder, study, and examine. With Naish, you put the project together, check it, and launch it. Relative to his marketing approach, Naish has coined the phrase "Fire, Aim, Fire." The first "Fire" represents dreaming up the marketing idea and launching it. When the responses start to come in, modify the idea as needed. That's the "Aim." And, of course, launch it again. That's another round of "Fire." Thus the moniker "Fire, Aim, Fire."

Naish is not the most patient guy around. He wants things done right now. As an example, back in January of 2011, I sent Naish an e-mail outlining the tasks I expected to accomplish in the first quarter of the year. It contained all sorts of things like tune-up the employee manuals, modify specific pages of the website, update the curriculum as needed, negotiate a couple of vendor contracts, etc. Almost exactly a week later, I called Naish on another matter. He asked how I was doing on my list. I told him the list was fine, meaning that I had included every relevant item I could think of. He rephrased his question "Is everything on your list done?" I said "What? Hell no. I haven't even started! Some of these items will take months to complete." He growled "Then you are already running behind."

When Naish comes up with an idea, he gathers his guys to create a plan, and then gives the green light to implement it. Thirty minutes later, he wants to know what progress has been made. Sixty minutes later he wants to know what the holdup is. You get the idea. The old saying is "If you want to get something done right away, give it to a busy man." In the spirit of true one-upmanship, if you want to get something done yesterday, give it to Naish Piazza. His tombstone will read: "Here lies Ignatius Piazza. Thanks for visiting, now get back to work!"

Naish Piazza is certainly not bashful. Regardless of social norms or taboos, Naish will tell you exactly what he thinks. I once watched Naish send one of our Range Masters to the back of the classroom to sit alone during a staff meeting. This was just exactly like when your parents sent you to your room…without dinner…to think about what you had done! Naish flat told him "If you are going to act like a child, I am going to treat you like a child." Additionally, Naish knows exactly what he wants. He is quick to determine if a proposal fits with the Front Sight way or not. If the issue at hand doesn't match his expectations, he will say so immediately. As such, some people feel Naish is too direct. Yet, you never have to wonder where you stand with Naish Piazza.

As you can imagine, Naish values loyalty. When he feels someone is loyal to him and Front Sight, Naish will back that person to the very end. Conversely, if Naish feels you are untrustworthy or represent a threat to the organization, say your goodbyes. Even if that person works diligently to get back in the "good graces," it will likely never happen. Naish has an iron clad memory for such things.

Naish is an excellent shooter, as you would assume. Back in August of 1993 he passed the very lofty 4-Weapons Combat Master Test and the Handgun Combat Master Test. 1993 was a long time ago and I am sure Naish's skills are less refined than they were two decades ago. However, even with a little rust, Naish Piazza would be a formidable foe.

Okay, so Naish is a hard worker, smart, well spoken, and demanding. As you can imagine with such a Type A personality, Naish can sometimes be a pain in the ass to work for. The same has been said of Steve Jobs and Donald Trump and George Patton; and look at what those guys accomplished. I am not suggesting that Front Sight rivals Apple or the U.S. military. But, I am saying that the leaders of those organizations have a good bit in common. You don't change the world by being a pansy.

What was it like working with Jeff Cooper?

Succinctly put, working under Jeff Cooper was terrific. I was young, green, and enthusiastic. Jeff was aristocratic, accomplished, worldly, and intelligent. This was a perfect match and Jeff served unwittingly as my mentor for years.

Jeff Cooper (right) giving Brad Ackman some friendly advice in the early years.

Jeff and his wife Janelle were the best, most sincere hosts I have ever encountered. I however, was not always the best guest. On one occasion back in 1989, I was teaching a handgun course with esteemed Range Master Ed Stock. Ed picked me up at the Phoenix airport in his Jeep CJ-5...with the top off...in August. He loved the heat and took pride in it. Not me. Roll up the windows and turn on the air conditioner. Anyway, the two-hour trek to Gunsite seemed like four in that miserable contraption.

Upon arrival at Gunsite, we checked in with Mrs. Cooper to learn where we would be staying for the week. As was the norm, Janelle placed Ed and me in the spare bedroom in the Cooper's home. This was a real luxury and I came to relish Janelle's hospitality. Janelle personally made breakfast, lunch, and dinner for her favorite staff. Yes, yes, thank you; that included me!

The next day was the start of the handgun course. The morning session ended uneventfully and lunch was excellent, as usual. After lunch, Ed and I headed back to the range. However, I got there without my sunglasses, which I had left back at the Cooper's home. Since our range was a fair distance from the Cooper's, Ed told me to take his Jeep. I pulled up into the Cooper's gravel driveway, right next to the open garage door. I put the Jeep in neutral, left the engine running, and ran inside to get my sunglasses from the lunch table. "Never mind me, I'm just grabbing my sunglasses," I hollered to Mrs. Cooper. I jumped right back into the Jeep, put it in gear and eased out the clutch. The vehicle rocked forward a bit, but didn't really move much. The gravel was pretty deep right there so I gunned it a little more. This time the Jeep felt like it was trying to roll OVER something. That was odd because I was on a flat driveway. So, I really gave it hell, which is when I heard a distinct canine yelp. Holy shit! I shut off the engine and looked underneath. There, just forward of the rear tire, was the Cooper's family dog, Gina. Gina was a good-sized hound, maybe 70 pounds or so, but she was old, tired, and fragile. And I just tried to run her over with Ed's Jeep! Truth be told, I must have rolled the tires up onto Gina a fair amount. The only reason I didn't drive right over her was the loose, deep gravel.

"Mrs. Cooper, I'm back...but I have a little problem!" I was carrying Gina in my arms and by now she was whining loudly. I really felt bad for Gina but I was equally worried about my own fate. I could just see where this was going: Gina was going to die, Janelle was going to be crushed, and I was going to hold the record for the shortest career as a Gunsite instructor. Mrs. Cooper gasped and then dashed back into the house for a blanket. She spread the blanket on the rear seat of her car and I laid Gina on it. Final resting place, I thought. Mrs. Cooper must have seen "CONCERN" written all over my face and she said "It's going to be alright." I had my doubts, but she headed to the vet and I headed back to the range. At about 3:00 that afternoon, I asked Ed if I could drive back to the Cooper's to check in, and apologize yet again. I saw Janelle's car was back...already. Oh God, that either means Gina was a goner or she was alright and didn't need any treatment at all. As old as that mutt was, she probably expired on the way to town. I braced myself for the tears and the tongue lashing, but I got neither. Gina was, in fact, okay. "She is going to be just fine," Mrs. Cooper said. "Would you like some iced tea?" Indeed I would; it's 95° out there and the dog is going to be fine. Hell yeah, let's celebrate with some iced tea! "No ma'am," I said. "I've got to get back to the students on my range; thank you though."

Man, did I ever dodge a bullet there. A lot can happen in 30 seconds; like a dog can walk out of the garage and curl up under a Jeep for some shade.

Jeff Cooper was very generous with his time and his conversation. You could ask Jeff anything at anytime. He was happy to tell you whatever he knew on the subject. I found him genuinely approachable.

Jeff was also very generous with his material items. If you looked longingly at the commemorative Bren Ten pistol on the fireplace mantle, Jeff would suggest you take it out and shoot it. If you wanted to understand the difference between .458 Winchester Magnum and .460 G&A, Jeff would walk downstairs to the Armory, grab both rifles and a couple boxes of ammo, and send you to the range to experiment for yourself.

Back in 1988 when I was living in Montana, Jeff and I had a philosophical discussion about elk hunting in the Bob

Marshall Wilderness. He asked me what rifle I was hunting with and I told him about the pre-1964 .270 Winchester my dad gave me. Jeff acknowledged that my rifle was sufficient, but proclaimed the proper rifle for Montana was a "Super Scout" in .350 Remington Magnum. It hits much harder and is far handier than that old Winchester. He was so adamant on the issue that he gave me his original "Super Scout 1." That's what I call putting your money where your mouth is.

Super Scout 1 is built on a Remington 660 Mohawk action and I hunted with that rifle for years before I decided to refurbish it. I replaced a few damaged and worn parts, swapped the old wood stock for a new Kevlar version, did some custom engraving, and then had it plated with hard chrome to better withstand the elements. In late-September of 2006, I had just received Super Scout 1 back from the hard chrome company and was reassembling it in my garage. My phone rang so I cradled the rifle in my left hand and picked up the phone with my right. It was a friend of mine in Arizona who announced to me "Jeff Cooper died today."

I know Jeff would want me to shoot that rifle until it absolutely fell apart but I can't bring myself to do that. I have not fired a single round through that rifle since September of 2006.

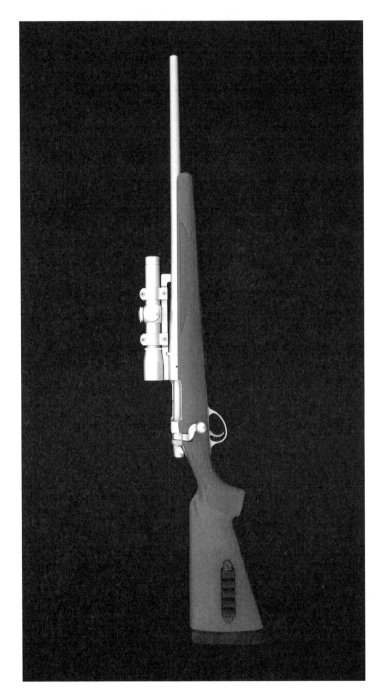

The rifle known as "Super Scout 1" given to me by Jeff Cooper in 1988 and refurbished in September 2006.

The Remington 660 Mohawk action left a good bit to be desired but it served nicely as a platform for the early Scout rifles.

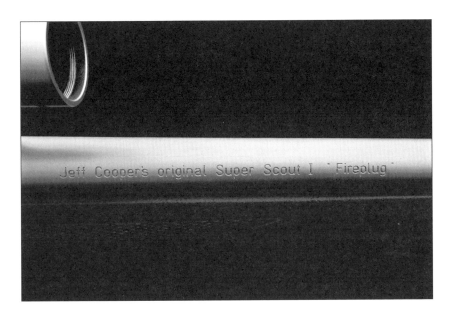

Engraving on the barrel of Jeff Cooper's original Super Scout 1. Jeff dubbed the .350 Remington Magnum cartridge "Fireplug" because of its short, stout profile.

For this custom engraving on the trigger guard, I simply copied a portion of the letter Jeff Cooper sent along with the rifle back in 1988.

Jeff Cooper was at his finest in the realms of literature, poetry, history, combat through the ages, hunting, metallurgy, exquisite swords, fine cuisine, and politics. He was well versed in each, and the dinner conversation usually proved that fact.

Jeff had inherently high expectations of everyone around him. He flat expected that everyone knew the engineering behind the Autobahn, the gear ratio of a Porsche 356 Speedster, the proper bullet selection for the .350 Remington Magnum if lion was on the agenda, which local wines best complimented the cuisine in and around Johannesburg, why the metallurgy of the Spanish swords in the first century BC was superior to that of the Romans, which sonnet was Shakespeare's finest and why, and how de Tocqueville influenced the modern view of classical liberalism.

Needless to say, he left lots of people behind, me included. Trying to keep intellectual pace with Jeff Cooper was like trying to play tennis with Pete Sampras or chess with Bobby Fischer. I knew I was going to get my ass kicked but it was sure fun trying. Some people were really turned off by all of this and called Jeff arrogant, elitist, snobbish, and intimidating. I didn't see him that way and I can say with certainty that my IQ went up a little bit after each fireside chat with Jeff Cooper.

So, let's review. What's it been like working with some of the biggest names in the firearm training world? The short answer is: I have enjoyed it so much that I have made it my life's work.

Hit by a Bus

Even after more than 25 years, there is still a ton left for me to accomplish in the firearms training industry. I look forward to helping open even more Front Sight facilities and spreading our influence across the nation, and beyond. I look forward to perhaps writing another book. Most notably, I look forward to training thousands more of the good folks who want to keep their loved ones safe.

However, if I were hit by a bus today (which would surely please some people), I would die satisfied. I would be satisfied with a long career in an endeavor that I love. And, I would be satisfied that I have made a meaningful contribution to the firearms training world.

I have Jeff Cooper to thank for introducing me to the subject and giving me a chance. I have Naish Piazza to thank for paving the way and expanding the entire industry. I have a handful of knuckleheads to thank for showing me how NOT to do it. But mostly, I thank the thousands of students who put their trust in me.

Thanks for joining me on my maiden book voyage. Go do your thing, be safe, and stay in Condition Yellow.

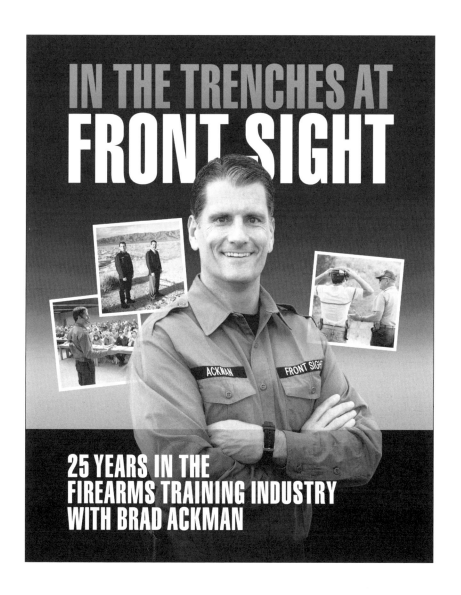

To order additional copies of Brad Ackman's

IN THE TRENCHES AT FRONT SIGHT

visit: RealDealPublications.com